A SURVEY OF VERB FORMS IN THE EASTERN UNITED STATES

A Survey of Verb Forms
in the
Eastern United States

E. Bagby Atwood

ANN ARBOR
THE UNIVERSITY OF MICHIGAN PRESS

Studies in American English 2

PREFACE

THE recent completion, in the Eastern States, of the field work for the Linguistic Atlas of the United States and Canada enables us to examine with some exactness the peculiarities of popular linguistic usage. Hans Kurath's volume, *A Word Geography of the Eastern United States* (Ann Arbor: University of Michigan Press, 1949), was the first extensive work based on this collection, and the striking nature of the results has made it highly desirable that other aspects of usage should be studied by drawing upon the same body of data. Though the Atlas materials are necessarily limited in geographical extent and in the number of informants used, they provide a systematic collection of information and make possible a factual, rather than a conjectural, type of exposition.

The present study, which confines itself to variant verb inflections, attempts to demonstrate such points as the following:

With regard to the verb, usage is rather sharply divided along social lines, more sharply than in vocabulary or in pronunciation. That is, nonstandard forms are most common among uneducated speakers in isolated communities, and are strikingly less frequent among the more highly educated. However, not even the usage of the most cultivated speakers is entirely free of such variants.

Although some nonstandard usages may well be national, or even international, in extent, a great many are clearly regional. With only a few exceptions the dissemination of these regional forms falls into the same pattern as that of the vocabulary. There are forms that are characteristic of the North (the New England settlements), the Midland (the Pennsylvania settlements), and the South (the plantation country). There are likewise forms that are characteristic of subdivisions of these areas—such as northeastern New England, the coastal South, the Virginia Piedmont, and the southern upland. This is not surprising, since grammatical forms as well as words and pronunciations are spread by migrations, by spoken and written communication within the several trade or culture areas, and by schooling and reading.

Thus the idea that there is a uniform grammar of the American "vulgate" must be abandoned. What we actually have is a variety of regional dialects, each with its own set of grammatical forms, as well as its peculiarities of pronunciation and vocabulary.

It is to be hoped that, in the present volume, the rather strict compression of data, the numerous abbreviations, and the space-saving stereotypes of expression will not conceal the intrinsic interest of the subject matter. Without much difficulty the linguist should be able to discover the materials that are pertinent to his purpose; the layman may observe many interesting grammatical changes; and even he who seeks only quaintness and humor in popular usage should be able to find these qualities.

I am deeply indebted to a number of persons for valuable aid in the preparation of this volume. Professor Hans Kurath, of the University of Michigan, not only made available to me the Linguistic Atlas collection, he also provided guidance in the methods of linguistic geography that could have come from no other person. Moreover, he more than once read the manuscript, made many valuable suggestions, and encouraged the publication of the work.   To Dr. Raven I. McDavid, Jr., I render thanks for patient and friendly help in sorting and using the latest of his field records, for the careful reading of the manuscript, and for checking, in the Atlas records, a number of items which it would have been impossible for me to examine at the time the volume went to press.   Mr. James Downer, of the University of Michigan, was of great service in supervising the conversion of my rough sketch maps into publishable charts, as well as in proofreading the final figures.   To my wife, Mary Bell Atwood, I am indebted for her patient work in typing, and occasionally correcting, the manuscript.

I wish to express my appreciation to the University of Michigan Press for its efficient handling of the task of publication—particularly to the staff of the Office of Scholarly Publications, for a most meticulous editing of the manuscript.   Finally, I am deeply indebted to the Research Institute of the University of Texas, which provided me a semester's relief from teaching duties for the study of linguistic geography, and which also granted a generous sum to the University of Michigan Press, thus helping to make possible the publication of the present volume.

E. B. A.

TABLE OF CONTENTS

Ask	Drag	Heat	Shrink
Begin	Draw	Help	Sit
Bite	Dream	Kneel	Spoil
Blow	Drink	Knit	Steal
Boil	Drive	Know	Sweat
Break	Drown	Learn	Swell
Bring	Eat	Lie	Swim
Burst	Fight	Might	Take
Buy	Fit	Plead	Teach
Catch	Freeze	Ride	Tear
Climb	Give	Ring	Throw
Come	Grow	Rise	Wake
Dive	Hang	Run	Wear
Do	Hear	See	Write

I says 'said'	He doesn't
I work, we work	What makes
I have	He looks like, favors, etc.
I be, he be, etc.	She rinses
He does	It costs

You were	Here are
We were	There are
People think	Oats are
They say	Cabbages are

Am not	Will not
Have not	Ought not
Was not	Dare not
Do not	Didn't use to

INTRODUCTION

IT HAS long been clear that some of the most striking differences between cultivated and popular speech are to be found in the conjugation of verbs, and there have been some very enlightening discussions of this feature of English morphology.[1] However, the unsystematic methods that have had to be applied in the collection of material or the inadequate geographical range of the observations often leaves us in doubt as to where certain forms occur, how frequent they are, or, for that matter, whether they actually occur at all in contemporary speech. The social distribution of the variant verb forms has never been adequately treated, so that we are often uncertain as to whether a reported form exists on the rustic level only, or whether it is also used by better-educated speakers in certain areas.

The materials that have been gathered for the Linguistic Atlas of the United States and Canada[2]

enable us to obtain a very accurate idea of the verb forms in use from Maine to eastern Georgia. The methods of field work need not be detailed here, since they are fully explained in the *Handbook of the Linguistic Geography of New England.*[3] It is sufficient to point out that all information was gathered in personal interviews by the use of standardized work sheets, or questionnaires. Thus a form that occurs in one community can be compared with the corresponding form in all the other communities that were investigated.

For the present study I have examined the Linguistic Atlas field records of something over 1,400 informants. Of these, 413 were gathered in New England, about 475 in the Middle Atlantic States, and about 550 in the South Atlantic States.[4] In New England the records were made by nine separate fieldworkers;[5] in the Middle Atlantic and the South Atlantic States as far as South Carolina nearly all of the interviewing was done by the late Dr. Guy S. Lowman. In South Carolina and Georgia and in northern and western New York, Dr. Raven I. McDavid, Jr., collected the bulk of the materials, though Lowman had previously made scattered records in these areas. Figure 1 shows the approximate locations of the communities in

---

[1] E.g., R. J. Menner, "The Verbs of the Vulgate," *American Speech,* I (1926), 230–40; Henry Alexander, "The Verbs of the Vulgate in Their Historical Relations," *American Speech,* IV (1929), 307–15; G. P. Krapp, *The English Language in America* (New York: Century, 1925), II, 257 ff.; H. L. Mencken, *The American Language,* 4th ed. (New York: Knopf, 1936), pp. 427–47, and *ibid., Supplement II* (1948), pp. 353–68. The various glossaries of Americanisms are more or less irregular in their treatment of verb forms; for example, R. H. Thornton, *An American Glossary* (2 vols.; London: Francis and Co., 1912; and a supplement in Vol. IV of *Dialect Notes*) gives rather full illustrations of some forms, such as *fit* for *fought,* but ignores others entirely. *The Dictionary of American English* (4 vols.; Chicago: Univ. Chicago Press, 1938–44) as a rule excludes verb morphology from consideration. Many word lists published in *American Speech, Dialect Notes,* and elsewhere have included nonstandard forms. Most of the material of this sort was collected in the *American Dialect Dictionary* (New York: Crowell, 1944) by Harold Wentworth. In the interest of consistency I have excluded from consideration all of this previously gathered material, since my entire procedure is based on a different type of data and a different method of collection. The results, however, should certainly be compared with those based on other methods. For a morphological analysis of standard American English verb forms, see B. Bloch, "English Verb Inflection," *Language,* XXIII (1947), 399–418.

[2] The New England materials were gathered from 1931

to 1933, and the finished maps were published as the *Linguistic Atlas of New England,* ed. Hans Kurath and Bernard Bloch (3 vols. in 6 parts; Providence, R. I.: Brown Univ., 1939–43). Materials for the Middle Atlantic States and the South Atlantic States have been gathered but not edited. See below.

[3] Ed. Hans Kurath and others (Providence, R. I.: Brown Univ., 1939).

[4] Some of the records are incomplete; moreover, in some communities a record may have been begun by one informant and completed or supplemented by another. Thus the number of records used is only approximate. The South Atlantic materials include records of 21 more or less primitive Negro informants gathered by Lowman; McDavid has added several more, including some examples of educated Negro speech. These records were always examined and are often commented on in this survey, but Negro usages are not entered on the maps.

[5] Bernard Bloch, Marguerite Chapallaz, Miles L. Hanley, Rachel S. Harris, Lee S. Hultzén, Martin Joos, Hans Kurath, Guy S. Lowman, Jr., and Cassil Reynard.

I

which the interviews were conducted.[6] The New England materials which I used are the edited sheets from which the maps in the *Linguistic Atlas of New England* were prepared;[7] the records for the remainder of the Eastern States are filed in unedited form in the Linguistic Atlas office at the University of Michigan. All of this material was made available to me during the sessions of the Linguistic Institute of 1946, and later during the fall of 1947 and the summers of 1948, 1949, and 1950, through the courtesy of Professor Hans Kurath, director of the Linguistic Atlas. Most of the McDavid records came in after this study was substantially complete. However, I have now examined all of these records and have included them in the present survey, though sometimes, no doubt, my comments on them may appear rather obviously to be later additions to the text.

TYPES OF INFORMANTS

It is particularly important to note the division of informants into types. In New England the informants have been arranged in three major groups (see *Handbook*, pp. 41–44): I, those of poor education; II, those of fair education; and III, those of superior education. These groups are further divided into A, aged, or old-fashioned, informants; and B, middle-aged or younger, hence more modern, informants. Most (but not all) of Type III are designated as "cultured."[8] In the Middle Atlantic and the South Atlantic States it is feasible at present to divide the informants into only three groups: I, older, old-fashioned, poorly educated; II, younger, more modern, better educated; and III, cultured. Lowman's usual practice was to interview in each community a clear-cut representative of rustic

(Type I) usage and one of modern (Type II) usage, and a cultured representative in certain key communities. His types are rather sharply distinguished, as a rule. Many of his Type I informants, particularly in the South Atlantic States, are described as "illiterate" but "intelligent," and he frequently went into the most isolated and backward communities to interview them, whereas the Type II group seem representative of the average half-educated inhabitant of the average community. McDavid's informants sometimes tend to shade gradually from Type I to Type II; moreover, he was unable, partly because of transportation difficulties, to interview quite so primitive a group of Type I informants as Lowman did. (For additional comments on this problem, see "Evaluation of Data," in the Conclusion, pp. 37–38.)

I have been able to check the classification into types of most of the South Atlantic informants and of some of those in the Middle Atlantic States with the fieldworkers' data on the age, education, occupation, and social contacts of each individual; for the remainder I have relied on the fieldworkers' assignments of informants to types. Thus, outside of New England, the arrangement of informants in types is tentative, and some individuals may ultimately be reclassified; however, considering the systematic methods used in selecting informants, I believe the arrangement to be fairly accurate.

It should be remembered that the classifications are to a great extent relative. That is, one Type I informant may be far more old-fashioned in his speech than another in the same area; moreover, in some areas Type I speech is much more rustic than in others. In some areas there is little difference between Types I and II in the choice of forms; in others the two show striking contrasts.[9]

Cultured informants are not very numerous, but they were carefully chosen to represent the different areas and types of society, and thus are sufficient to warrant conclusions as to the cultivated usage of the East. There are records of 41 cultured in-

---

[6] Each "point" on this map represents a small area (usually a township in New England, a county in the Middle Atlantic and the South Atlantic States). Two informants were generally interviewed at each "point"— though in the larger cities a good many more records were made (e.g., 13 in New York, nine in Brooklyn, eight in Philadelphia, six in Baltimore).

[7] The tabulations and the maps should therefore correspond to the published maps of the *Atlas*, except for the elimination of certain types of responses. See below, p. 3.

[8] On the criteria for the selection of cultured informants, see *Handbook*, pp. 41–44. Needless to say, not all of this group are the metropolitan type; a good many represent local and rural cultured speech, which often preserves certain archaic traits of the region.

[9] Probably the usage of Type II would be closest to most writers' ideas of "vulgate" or "the common speech." It should be remembered, however, that speakers of the more rustic type (I) are far from rare in many large areas of the United States; they are not only numerous, but constitute a considerable social and political force, as any Southern politician knows.

formants[10] in New England and of about 50, each, in the Middle Atlantic and the South Atlantic States.

PROCEDURE AND TERMINOLOGY

In tabulating the responses to the various items on the worksheets I have recorded only *spontaneous* occurrences of the verb forms, never those reported by the informant as "heard from others," "formerly used," "used by the uneducated," and so on. I have also eliminated "suggested" forms. If, for example, the fieldworker by indirect questioning elicits from the informant the preterite form *clum* /klʌm/ for *climbed*, or if he catches *clum* in the unguarded conversation of the informant, this is entered as an "occurrence" of the form; if, on the other hand, the fieldworker actually uses the form *clum* and asks whether or not it is used by the informant, the response is not entered as an "occurrence," even though the informant may agree that the form is natural to him. As a result of this procedure, I believe it is legitimate to conclude that the non-standard verb forms are at least as frequent in popular speech as my tabulations show them to be. In some areas, particularly, they are probably more frequent, since, no matter how skillful a fieldworker may be, there are many informants who hesitate to use a form that is perfectly natural to them because they feel that it might be disapproved as "incorrect."

I have tried to keep the geographical terminology as simple as possible. Lower-case abbreviations are used for directions: e.g., "s.w. Pa." for "southwestern Pennsylvania" and "e. c. N. C." for "east central North Carolina." New England (N. Eng.) includes a few communities in New Brunswick as well as all of Maine (Me.), New Hampshire (N. H.), Vermont (Vt.), Massachusetts (Mass.), Rhode Island (R. I.), and Connecticut (Conn.). The Middle Atlantic States (M. A. S.) include New York (N. Y.), New Jersey (N. J.), Pennsylvania (Pa.), eastern Ohio (O.), and West Virginia (W. Va.).[11] The South Atlantic States (S. A. S.)

include Delaware (Del.), Maryland (Md.), Virginia (Va.), North Carolina (N. C.), South Carolina (S. C.), and approximately the eastern half of Georgia (Ga.).

The term "Eastern New England" is used as in the *Handbook;* in addition, it is convenient to refer to "Northeastern New England," which includes all of Maine and New Hampshire, all but the western-most tier of counties in Vermont, and Essex County in northeastern Massachusetts. I follow Professor Kurath[12] in using the term "Midland" to refer to what is roughly the Pennsylvania settlement area, including all of Pennsylvania except the northern one fourth, at least the southern part of New Jersey ("West Jersey"), western Maryland, West Virginia, and those portions of Virginia lying to the west of the Blue Ridge. The term "South Midland" applies to the mountainous territory beginning approximately at the valley of the Kanawha in West Virginia and extending southward to take in south-western Virginia and western North Carolina. By "the South" I mean the speech area comprising the southern coastal plain and Piedmont, as delimited by Kurath.[13] "Eastern Virginia" means all of Virginia east of the Blue Ridge. "Piedmont Virginia" indicates this same territory without the points of land along the coast known as the "Tidewater" area. "Delmarva" is applied to the peninsula containing Delaware and the Eastern Shores of Maryland and Virginia. Of course, the principal mountains, rivers, river valleys, and cities are also referred to.

In the verb forms that are analyzed I have nearly always used traditional dialect spellings, though I have sometimes improvised spellings in the conventional alphabet. However, I have also followed each form with pronunciation symbols between slanting lines, thus: *mought* /maut/. I believe that these symbols represent phonemes—there would be no point in indicating subphonemic features in a study of morphological types. The impossibility of making a phonemic analysis of every area of the

---

[10] I.e., Type III informants. In the *Handbook* 43 informants are designated as cultured, since some of Type II are put in that category.

[11] Actually, in the Linguistic Atlas survey the southern one fourth of New Jersey and the eastern end of West Virginia are included in the South Atlantic States, for

cartographic reasons. In the present study, however, purely for convenience, I have included all of New Jersey and West Virginia in the Middle Atlantic States. The survey in Ohio includes only the easternmost tier of counties and a few communities in the southern part of the state, along the Ohio River.

[12] *A Word Geography of the Eastern United States* (Ann Arbor, Mich.: Univ. Michigan Press, 1949), pp. 27-37.

[13] *Ibid.*, pp. 37-47.

East (ideally, every informant should be analyzed)[14] prevents absolute certainty as to the phonemic distinctiveness of every form recorded. In general, however, I believe that forms designated by different sets of symbols are different phonemically and therefore morphologically—the preterite *burst* /bɜst/ is a different speech form from the preterite *bust* /bʌst/, whether the /ɜ/ occurs without "*r*-quality" or with such quality, whether it occurs as a phonetic monophthong or as a diphthong [ɜɪ], [ʌɝ], and so on. The alphabet used in the transcriptions is based on the International Phonetic Alphabet and, more directly, on the alphabet of the Linguistic Atlas (*Handbook*, pp. 122–43). Its similarity to the fairly well known system of Kenyon and Knott[15] should result in its ready comprehension by the general reader.[16]

The ensuing survey is concerned with: I, tense forms; II, personal forms of the present indicative; III, number and concord;[17] IV, negative forms; V, infinitive and present participle; and VI, phrases. Matters of purely phonetic or phonemic interest—i.e., without morphological significance—have as a rule been excluded. I am concerned here chiefly with present-day distribution and will for the most part defer the historical interpretation of the various forms.

I have attempted to show the approximate frequency of the verb forms by means of rather simplified fractions—"two thirds," "nine tenths," and so on. I thought that reduction to decimals would be useless and would give a false air of exactitude, since in the completed Linguistic Atlas no doubt some records that I have examined will be eliminated. Still, I feel that the estimates of relative frequency are comparatively accurate and that they provide a much better guide to current usage than any amount of random observation could give. Occasionally I use such a formula as 37/176, which would mean that, according to my count, 37 out of a total of 176 informants in a certain area, or of a certain type (as the context will make clear), use a certain form.[18]

---

[14] For a phonemic analysis of one type of northeastern English, see B. Bloch and G. L. Trager, "The Syllabic Phonemes of English," *Language*, XVII (1941), 223–46, and *Outline of Linguistic Analysis* (Baltimore: Linguistic Society, 1942). An interesting attempt to extend the same principle of analysis to other varieties of American English is made in G. L. Trager and Henry L. Smith, *An Outline of English Structure: Studies in Linguistics, Occasional Papers* 3 (Norman, Okla.: Battenburg Press, 1951). For a different view of English phonemic structure, see Kenneth L. Pike, *Phonemics* (Ann Arbor, Mich.: Univ. Michigan Press, 1947).

[15] *A Pronouncing Dictionary of American English* (Springfield, Mass.: G. and C. Merriam Co., 1944).

[16] It seems to me impossible to devise a set of symbols that are completely satisfactory for all the speech areas and all the social levels of the East. My purpose is merely to show, for example, that *mought* is pronounced like *out*, not like *bought*—without attempting to indicate the numerous variants in the vowels of *out* and *bought* that occur in the East. Daniel Jones would call this system "diaphonic" rather than "phonemic." The vowel symbols used in this study, with examples from "standard" usage, are: /i/, *see*; /ɪ/, *bit*; /e/, *taken*; /ɛ/, *set*; /æ/, *ran*; /ɑ/, *hot*; /ɔ/, *taught*; /o/, *rode*; /ʊ/, *took*; /u/, *threw*; /ʌ/, *run*; /ɜ/, *burst*; /ə/, *awoke* (unstressed vowel). The final sounds in *catch* and *ridge* are written /tʃ/ and /dʒ/. Inflectional -*en* is consistently transcribed /ən/, though it takes various phonetic shapes: [ən], [n̩], [ŋ̍], and so on. Syllabic -*ed* is consistently transcribed /əd/, though it may

be phonetically [əd], [ɛd], or [ɪd]. The same method is used for -*es*. Words with historical postvocalic *r* are regularly written with /r/ (e.g., /worn/), though in some dialects the /r/ may not be present and in others it may appear as [ə] or as vowel length.

[17] The distinction made in this survey between person and number is to a great extent arbitrary and a matter of convenience. Often, of course, the same inflectional form (e.g., *does*) signifies both person and number, as well as tense and mood.

[18] Where such a formula is used, it applies only to the New England records and to the records in other areas gathered by Lowman. The records recently gathered by McDavid are not yet classified in a way that permits this sort of tabulation. However, when forms in the McDavid records show appreciable differences in frequency from those in other records, I have attempted to indicate the fact.

VERB FORMS IN THE EASTERN UNITED STATES

I. TENSE FORMS

Ask (104)[1]

In the M. A. S. and the S. A. S. the present infinitive and the preterite forms are recorded in the contexts "I am going to (ask) him" and "I (asked) him."[2]

As a present form, *ask* /æsk/ strongly predominates in all the larger areas, the variants being confined to less than one seventh of the informants in the M. A. S. and less than one third in the S. A. S. *Ask* is universal among cultured informants.

The present *ast* /æst/ is scattered through the M. A. S. (except N. Y. and n. N. J.) and the S. A. S., reaching something like concentration in s. N. J. and n.e. N. C. Nearly one sixth of the Eastern informants use this form.

The present form *ax* /æks/ does not occur north of the Pa.-Md. boundary, and is found only at a few isolated points in W. Va., Md., and Va. (see Figure 2, where the preterite forms of *ax* are shown).[3] In N. C. this form becomes much more common, reaching considerable concentration in the western one fourth of the state, where nearly all of the Type I informants use it.

In forming the preterite, most (at least five sixths) of the M. A. S. informants use the combination *ask* : *asked*[4] /æskt/. In the S. A. S. this combination is confined to a minority of informants, though it is almost universal in cultured speech.

The leveled[5] combination *ask* : *ask* occurs in a very scattered way in Pa. and Md., and becomes fairly common in Va., where more than one fourth of the noncultured informants use it. It is also in use, though less commonly, in N. C. and S. C.

The combination *ask* : *ast* is recorded only a few times in the M. A. S., but becomes very common in s. Md. and Va., being used by about one third of the informants in these areas. In N. C. and S. C. the forms are considerably less frequent.

Those who use the present *ast* (see above) almost invariably use the same form as a preterite.

Those who use the present *ax* nearly always inflect it regularly (i.e., /ækst/), though there are four instances of the leveled combination *ax* : *ax*.

In S. C. and e. Ga., where McDavid frequently recorded *ask(ed)* in other contexts than before *him*, the form /æs/ is common before consonants, as in "ask(ed) /æs/ me about it." The same form is occasionally recorded in n. and w. N. Y.

---

[1] The numbers following the verbs in this study correspond to the pages of the work sheets. See *Handbook of the Linguistic Geography of New England*, ed. Hans Kurath and others (Providence, R. I.: Brown Univ., 1939), pp. 149–58.

The work sheets for the Middle Atlantic and the South Atlantic States, as yet unpublished, differ from those for New England in that (1) p. 104 has been added; (2) the number of questions on pp. 1, 7, 55, and 60 has been increased, so that these pages have become 1 and 1A, 7 and 7A, 55 and 55A, 60 and 60A; (3) a few items have been added, omitted, or transferred from one page to another.

The text always indicates whether a term was investigated in only a part of the Eastern United States. If a term does not occur in the *Linguistic Atlas of New England* (ed. Hans Kurath and Bernard Bloch; 3 vols. in 6 parts; Providence, R. I.: Brown Univ., 1939–43), or if its location in the work sheets has been shifted, the page number refers to the work sheets for the Middle Atlantic and the South Atlantic States.

[2] In this and most other morphological items McDavid picked up the required form in conversation, regardless of the precise context in which it occurred.

[3] In the maps which are presented in this survey each symbol represents the spontaneous occurrence of a form in the speech of one informant. By reference to the base map (Figure 1), one may obtain a fair idea of the frequency of the occurrences in a given area. Northern Me., for which material is available, has been cut off in the preparation of the maps. In maps where shading is used, shaded areas designate the presence of a form in most or nearly all communities. Where a form is missing from only one or two communities, such areas are disregarded in the shading

(i.e., they are not left unshaded) provided the form occurs on all sides of these communities. Isoglosses (lines indicating the outer limits of forms) have generally been somewhat simplified by disregarding isolated instances. Unusually large symbols, which are sometimes used on the maps to prevent overcrowding, indicate that a form is in very common use in a given area. See also the note on the figures, p. 46.

[4] The colon is used to designate combinations of present and preterite forms; the hyphen designates combinations of preterite and past participle.

Note that the preterite forms *ask* and *ast* may be merely mechanical phonetic simplifications rather than morphological variations. Since, however, the inflectional /-t/ is not normally lost (see below, p. 44), I have included both of these among the verb "forms."

[5] I use "leveled" to indicate the use of identical forms for the present and the preterite or for the preterite and the past participle. Such preterite forms as *ask* and *sweat* are referred to as "uninflected"—i.e., uninflected for tense. "Inflected by means of zero" might be substituted for "uninflected," if one prefers; however, I see no particular advantage in this terminology for our purposes.

There is little difference between Types I and II in the choice of forms of this verb, except that *ax* and *axed* are almost exclusively Type I forms. They are often reported by informants in all parts of the S. A. S. as "old" or "old-fashioned" though still in use.

Begin (102)

The preterite is recorded in the context "He (began) to talk."

The frequency of the preterite forms cannot be determined because a rather large number of informants in all areas choose the verb *commence*, and a number of others use the preterite of *start*.

The form *begun* /bi'gʌn/ occurs in about half the communities in N. Eng. and in something less than half in most other areas. It is slightly more common in Type I than in Type II, but the difference is not very great.

The uninflected *begin* /bi'gɪn/ occurs in only seven N. Eng. communities, including four contiguous ones in s. c. Vt. In most of the M. A. S. this form is also quite rare, but it becomes more common in the S. A. S., occurring more often than *begun* in e. Va.

Bite (33)

The past participle is recorded in the context "He was (bitten) by a dog."

The form *bitten* /bɪtən/ is strongly favored by cultured informants everywhere. Moreover, in N. Eng. it is used by a majority of the noncultured in all types except IA. Elsewhere in the East *bitten* is rather sharply limited by the variants to be mentioned.

Bit /bɪt/ is used by a slight majority of Type IA informants in N. Eng., and by from one fourth to one third of the other noncultured types. It is also current, but not very common (6/41), in cultivated speech. Elsewhere in the Eastern States, except possibly around New York City, *bit* predominates very heavily in Type I, and a little less heavily in Type II. Most Southern Negroes use this form, though two use *bite* /bait/ : "got bite."

An interesting geographical phenomenon is the compound *dogbit* ("he was dogbit," or "he got dogbit"), which covers the South Midland and adjoining parts of the South (see Figure 3). In W. Va. south of the Kanawha and in s.w. Va. it is practically universal; it reaches north to s.w. Pa. and southeast to the Atlantic in the Peedee and Cape Fear valleys. It is fairly common in the inland portions of S. C. and e. Ga.

Blow (6)

The preterite is recorded in the context "The wind (blew) hard."

Two forms are current, *blew* /blu/ and *blowed* /blod/. *Blew* predominates among all types throughout most of s. N. Eng. and the M. A. S. (except s. and e. W. Va.). Its currency elsewhere may be deduced from the extent of *blowed*.

Blowed occurs with some frequency in n.e. N. Eng., where it is used by more than half of Types IA and IB and by about one third each of Types IIA and IIB. The remaining occurrences in N. Eng. are scattered through e. Mass., R. I., and e. Conn. *Blowed* is almost lacking in w. N. Eng., e. N. Y., n. N. J., and n. and e. Pa., though it is reasonably common in n. and w. N. Y. As we proceed southward from c. Pa., *blowed* becomes more and more frequent until in N. C. it is used by more than nine tenths of Type I and by about four fifths of Type II. Throughout the S. A. S. *blowed* is just about universal in Type I and predominates, though less strongly (86/145), in Type II as well. Only one cultured informant (W. Va.) uses this form.

Boil (46)

The past participle (adjective) form is recorded in the context "(boiled) eggs."

The form *boiled* /bɔild/ is universal in N. Eng. and nearly so in N. Y., n. N. J., and n. Pa. Elsewhere it more or less heavily predominates in Type II, but it is somewhat limited in Type I in certain areas, as will appear.

The form with voiceless suffix, *boilt* /bɔilt/ or (occasionally among Type I informants) /bailt/, is most characteristic of the Midland area (s. Pa., w. Md., and W. Va.), reaching its greatest frequency in W. Va., where about three fifths of all informants use it. This form also occurs, though much less frequently, in all parts of the S. A. S., showing some concentration in w. c. N. C. It is rare in S. C. and Ga. In both the M. A. S. and the S. A. S. more than three fourths of the occurrences of *boilt* are among Type I informants.

Break (48)

In the M. A. S. and the S. A. S. the past participle is recorded in the context "The glass is (broken)."

Broken /brokən/ is in use in all areas; it is almost universal in cultured speech, and predominates in Type II speech.

Broke /brok/ predominates in Type I speech in all areas except the New York City area, where it occurs only in scattered fashion. Roughly, two thirds of the Type I informants in the M. A. S. and the S. A. S. use this form, as well as about one third of the Type II informants. Only four cultured informants in the East use *broke* in this context.

Bring (27)

The past participle is recorded in the context "I have (brought) your coat."

Brought /brɔt/ is very heavily predominant in all major areas among all classes.

Brung /brʌŋ/ occurs in very scattered fashion throughout the Eastern States. There are 51 occurrences divided among N. Eng., N. Y., N. J., Pa., O., W. Va., Va., N. C., S. C., and Ga. Nothing like a geographical concentration is evident except possibly in n.w. Pa., where this form occurs in several contiguous communities. It is dominantly a Type I form, but in Pa. and W. Va. almost as many Type II informants use it.

One N. Eng. informant uses *broughten* /brɔtən/, and a few Southern Negroes say *done bring*.

Burst (18)

The preterite is recorded in the context "The pipe (burst)." The variant preterite forms of course presuppose two present tense forms, *burst* /bɜst/ and *bust* /bʌst/.

The form *burst* strongly predominates among all types throughout N. Eng.; more than three fourths of all informants use this form alone or alongside some variant. *Burst* is almost universal around New York City, and predominates among Type II informants in all areas except parts of the South Midland, particularly s. W. Va. It is very strongly preferred by cultured informants in all areas.

Bursted /bɜstəd/ occurs among a relatively small group of N. Eng. informants (44/413), most of whom (32) fall in Types IA and IIA, with no particular geographical concentration. Elsewhere in the East *bursted* is more characteristic of Type II, being used by something like from one fourth to one half of this group. Twelve cultured informants, mostly scattered through the S. A. S., use *bursted*.

Bust /bʌst/ appears in more or less scattered fashion in all major areas, almost exclusively among informants of Type I. This form appears most frequently in the German area of Pa. and throughout N. C., where more than one fourth of Type I informants use it.

Busted /bʌstəd/, which is often thought to be the universal popular form, is actually used by a minority of informants of all types in nearly all areas.[6] It predominates in Type I only in N. C. and S. C., where slightly over half of this group use it.

With regard to the social distribution of these forms, it should be noted that the cleavage is much more sharp in some areas than in others. In N. Eng., although *bust* is almost entirely confined to the A types, *busted* shows no very great variation among the noncultured types. The most interesting contrast between rustic and modern usage is in N. C., where 61 of 74 Type I informants use *bust* or *busted*, whereas 52 of 57 Type II informants use *burst* or *bursted*.

It should be remembered that this verb is recorded only with the literal meaning 'spring apart.' In some of its figurative and slang meanings, *bust* is probably to be regarded as a separate word, whose forms may have a completely different distribution.

Buy (45)

The attributive past participle (adjective) is attested sporadically in the expression *bought* or *boughten bread*, a lexical variant of "baker's bread."

In N. Eng. there are 57 occurrences of *boughten* /bɔtən/ as against only two of *bought* /bɔt/. The occurrences of *boughten* are mostly concentrated in n.e. N. Eng., particularly the Merrimack Valley and s. Me. This form is somewhat more characteristic of the older types (IA, IIA, IIIA) than of the younger, though the difference is not striking. Five cultured informants (over one third of those who were interviewed in n.e. N. Eng.) use *boughten*.

---

[6] E.g., 72/413 in N. Eng., 26/153 in Pa., 25/140 in Va.

In the M. A. S. *boughten* is about twice as frequent as *bought,* though both forms are very uncommon in this context (being used by about one tenth of the informants). Type I informants account for three fourths of the occurrences of *boughten,* while *bought* is found mainly among Type II (and cultured) informants.

In the S. A. S. Lowman did not usually record the attributive form of the past participle of *buy,* but McDavid elicited it from a good many informants. In Lowman's data *boughten* occurs only in a few communities in N. C.; McDavid found only two instances of *boughten* in S. C. and Ga., as against 71 of *bought.*

No cultured informant in the M. A. S. or the S. A. S. uses *boughten.*

Catch (98)

The preterite is recorded in the context "Who (caught) it?"

The standard[7] *caught* /kɔt/ is dominant in all areas among all classes, though limited in Type I as will be indicated.

The weak preterite *catched,* almost always pronounced /kɛtʃt/, occurs in both n.e. and s.w. N. Eng., though it is nearly, or entirely, lacking in most communities in e. Mass and w. Vt. Frequencies vary from about one fourth of Type IA to about one eighth of Type IIB. A great many of these informants also use *caught.*

Elsewhere in the Eastern States *catched* occurs in all major areas (see Figure 4). It is somewhat rare in N. Y. (10 occurrences), but becomes considerably more common in the South and South Midland, occurring in nearly half the communities investigated in W. Va. and N. C. (much less commonly in S. C. and Ga.). Outside of N. Eng. *catched* is almost exclusively a rustic form, nearly nine tenths of the occurrences being found in Type I.

The pronunciation /kɪtʃt/, it will be noted, is very widely scattered except for parts of n.e. N. Eng.

The form *cotch* /katʃ/ occurs a few times around Chesapeake Bay as well as in w. N. C. and s.

---

[7] The term "standard" is used in a conventional and admittedly inexact sense throughout this study. Sometimes, as will be seen, the form usually regarded as standard does not actually predominate among cultured informants.

W. Va. Of the 14 informants in the S. A. S. who use this form, four are Negroes, eight are farmers 73 to 86 years of age, and two are women of 68.

Climb (96)

The preterite is recorded in the context "He (climbed) up a tree." In N. Eng., only, the past participle is also recorded in the context "I have often (climbed) up."

The preterite form *climbed* /klaimd/ is almost universal in the cultivated speech of all areas. In other types of speech it is limited by certain strong, or vowel-change, preterite forms, as indicated below.

In N. Eng. about half the informants use the strong preterite forms; there is no geographical concentration, though these forms are somewhat rare in e. R. I. and the Plymouth and Cape Cod areas. Something more than half the older informants (IA and IIA) use the strong forms; a little more than one third of the younger ones (IB and IIB) do so. Elsewhere in the East, except for part of n. N. J. and e. Pa. and the area around New York City, the strong forms are used by most Type I informants, the proportion ranging from about two thirds (N. Y.) to well over nine tenths (N. C.). The geographical distribution of the various strong preterite forms is shown in Figure 5. In N. Eng. (except Cape Cod), N. Y. (except the lower Hudson Valley), and the northernmost edge of Pa., the form *clim* /klɪm/ strongly predominates (i.e., by more than 10 to one) over the other strong forms. In the rest of Pa., as in N. J., w. Md., W. Va., and the Shenandoah Valley of Va., the form *clum* /klʌm/ is heavily favored, though in some communities *clim* likewise occurs. In the area around Chesapeake Bay, as on the points of land in Va. and in n.e. N. C. *clim* is the only strong form in use, whereas farther inland in the S. A. S. there is a considerable mixture. The Piedmont area of Va. (as well as some areas to the westward) is distinguished by the presence of *clome* /klom/ along with *clim* and *clum;* in inland N. C. *clum* and *clim* are about equally distributed, and there are a few occurrences of *clome.* In S. C. *clim* predominates along the coast, *clum* in the "upcountry."

There are seven occurrences of *cloom* /klum/, nearly all of which are in the Piedmont area of Va. and adjoining areas of N. C.

Clam /klæm/ is used by two N. Eng. and four Southern informants, two of whom are Negroes.

Clammed /klæmd/ (presumably with a present form *clam* /klæm/) is used by one N. Eng. and seven Southern informants, including four Negroes.

The uninflected *climb* /klaim/ is used by two Negro informants.

In N. Eng., where both preterite and past participle are recorded, there is no evidence of widespread differentiation of the two forms. A few informants give *climbed-clim* or *clim-climbed*, and two show the combination *clim-clum*. These combinations probably represent nothing more than hesitation between two current forms.

Come (102)

The preterite is recorded in the context "He (came) over to see me."

Came /kem/ predominates in all classes only in a small area around New York City, though it is heavily favored by cultured informants in all areas.

Come /kʌm/[8] occurs in nearly all the communities of N. Eng., being almost as common among younger informants as among the more old-fashioned. Elsewhere, outside of Greater New York City, *come* is used by from two thirds (N. Y.) to all (N. C.) of the Type I informants, whereas from one third (N. Y.) to seven eighths (N. C.) of the Type II informants use it. All Negro informants use *come*.

Dive (95)

The preterite is recorded in the context "He (dived) in."

The geographical distribution of the forms is indicated in Figure 6.

Dived /daivd/ is uncommon throughout N. Eng., N. Y., n. Pa., and e. N. J.; in this whole territory it is used by less than one out of 15 of the informants, without distinction as to type (about one eighth of the cultured informants in N. Eng. use it). In a belt in n. c. and e. Pa. and along the upper Ohio, *dived* and *dove* /dov/ occur about equally, the former being more common among older informants. Elsewhere in the M. A. S. and the S. A. S. to and including N. C., *dived* heavily predominates on all levels, being limited only by *div* (see below).

In the northeastern area indicated on the map *dove* is almost universal. Within the areas of divided usage the more modern informant uses *dove* in more than three fourths of the communities, and at least that proportion of cultured informants choose this form in these areas. There is not the slightest doubt that the area of *dove* is extending itself to the south and west.[9]

South of the Peedee in S. C. *dove* is also fairly common, and it has some currency in coastal Ga. In these areas it is quite frequent in urban and cultured speech, somewhat less so in rustic speech.

The form *div* /dɪv/ shows the typical distribution of an archaism, being most common in n.e. N. Eng. and the coastal and mountain areas of the South and the South Midland. About six out of seven of the informants who use it fall in Type I (or Types IA and IIA in N. Eng.), and three N. C. Negro informants use it.

There are five occurrences of *duv* /dʌv/, concentrated in s. N. J. near the mouth of the Delaware.

A few Negro informants use the uninflected *dive*.

Do (102)

In N. Eng., only, the preterite is recorded in the context "He (did) it last night."

Did is universal among cultured informants. Among the other types the form *done* /dʌn/ predominates rather strongly except in Mass. and R. I., where the two forms are about equally divided. *Done* is about as common among the more modern informants as among the more old-fashioned.

Drag (21)

In the M. A. S. and the S. A. S. (but not in N. Eng.) the preterite is recorded in the context "(dragged) a log."

Dragged /drægd/ predominates among cultured informants everywhere, but it predominates among the other types only in N. Y., n. Pa., e. Va., S. C., and Ga. Elsewhere in these types it is more or less narrowly limited by the competing form *drug* /drʌg/.

Drug occurs in the middle Hudson Valley, throughout N. J., in all of Pa. except the northern-

---

[8] Instances of the unstressed [kəm] are regarded as occurrences of *come*.

[9] Another characteristic of an advancing form is its appearance in the more populous centers ahead of the main line of advance (in this instance, the Pittsburgh, Baltimore, and Washington areas). Professor Robert Hall has applied the metaphor "parachuting" to this phenomenon.

most portion, in W. Va., and in almost all parts of the S. A. S. to and including N. C. It is somewhat limited in the Piedmont and Tidewater areas of Va., where only one third of Type I and one tenth of Type II informants use it; it is even less common in S. C. and e. Ga. Elsewhere it predominates rather strongly in Types I and II, being about as common in one as in the other. It has some currency in cultivated speech, particularly in the M. A. S. All together, 10 cultured informants in the M. A. S. and four in the S. A. S. use it.

Draw (104)

In the M. A. S. and the S. A. S. the preterite is recorded in the context "He (drew) it out."

Drew /dru/ predominates in cultivated speech and in Type II speech in all areas.

The weak form *drawed* /drɔd/ is very clearly rustic and rather rapidly receding. It is somewhat uncommon in e. N. Y. and N. J., being confined to less than one fourth of Type I; in n. and w. N. Y. and in Pa. a little less than half the informants of this type use it. To the southward it becomes more frequent, being used by nearly nine tenths of Type I informants in N. C. In Type II, *drawed* hardly occurs in e. N. Y. or N. J., and never reaches a frequency of more than one fourth in any area of the M. A. S. or the S. A. S.

One Negro informant uses the uninflected *draw* /drɔ/.

Dream (97)

The preterite is recorded in the context "I (dreamed) all night."

The form *dreamed* /drimd/ is used by about one third of the informants in the East, without any significant geographical concentration. It is slightly more frequent in W. Va. and O. than elsewhere, being used by nearly half the informants in those areas. The social distribution will be noted later.

The principal variant is *dreamt*. This nearly always shows the "intrusive" /p/, /drɛmpt/, and (particularly among Type I informants), more often than not, loss of final /t/, /drɛmp/.[10] This loss of the preterite affix is common everywhere, but particularly in the South and the South Mid-

---

[10] Note that this could hardly be assimilative loss of the final /t/, since in the context specified in the work sheets the verb is followed by a vowel.

land; e.g., in N. C. about four fifths of those who use *dreamt* drop the final /t/, /drɛmp/.

As has been implied, *dreamt* is used by the majority of speakers in all areas. Throughout N. Eng., N. Y., and N. J. there is nothing to indicate that it is an archaic or receding form; in communities of divided usage it occurs in the speech of the more modern informant at least as often as in that of the more old-fashioned. Fully three fourths of the cultured informants (all of those in New York City and Brooklyn) use *dreamt,* though some of these used *dreamed* as well. It appears that *dreamt* is at least holding its own and is probably gaining favor in the northern areas mentioned. In the remainder of the M. A. S. (Pa., W. Va., and O.), there is some little evidence of a change toward *dreamed* in popular speech; in about three fifths of the communities of divided usage this form is chosen by the younger informant. In these areas, too, however, *dreamt* is strongly favored (about two to one) by cultured informants. Throughout the S. A. S. *dreamt* is very clearly receding. In about seven eighths of the communities where usage is divided, the more modern informant chooses *dreamed.* Cultured usage, however, is just about evenly divided.

Throughout the East, it should be noted, an unusually large number of informants of all types use both *dreamt* and *dreamed.*

Fifteen or 20 informants, nearly all in N. C. and S. C., use /drɪmp/ and /drɪmpt/. This may be the result of the coalescence of the phonemes /ɛ/ and /ɪ/ before nasal consonants.

Other forms that occur in isolation from once to three times each are *dream* /drim/, *dramp* /dræmp/, *drump* /drʌmp/, and *dramed* /dremd/.

Drink (49)

The preterite and the past participle are recorded in the contexts "I (drank) a lot of it" and "How much have you (drunk)?"

The preterite *drank* /dræŋk/ very strongly predominates among all classes except as limited in certain areas by the variants to be mentioned.

The preterite *drunk* /drʌŋk/ is rare throughout the entire Northern area (N. Eng., N. Y., and n. Pa.), and occurrences (19) are widely scattered except in the lower Merrimack Valley and adjacent areas. It is also rare in the South from Chesapeake Bay to the Neuse River in N. C. In the Midland *drunk* is somewhat more frequent (see Figure 7), showing some regularity of occurrence in s. c. Pa., W. Va., and the western portions of Va., N. C., and S. C.; it also reaches to the coast in N. C. and S. C., particularly in the area between the Neuse and the Peedee. It is principally a Type I form, though used by a few Type II informants, chiefly in Pa. and W. Va.

The preterite *drinked* /drɪŋkt/ is considerably more frequent than *drunk* in N. Eng., being used by 61 informants, mostly in n.e. N. Eng. It shows most frequency in Type IA (34/120), but is by no means unknown in the other types. Elsewhere in the East, as the map indicates, there are scattered occurrences of *drinked* in all major areas. In the Tidewater areas of Va. and s. Md. it is about as frequent as any other form in Type I, while in the considerable area extending inland from n.e. N. C. it is almost the only form in use among informants of this type. It is also fairly frequent in S. C., except in the coastal settlements. Hardly any Type II informants outside of N. Eng. use this form, and no cultured informant uses it.

Something like a dozen informants in the S. A. S. and three or four in the M. A. S. use the uninflected preterite *drink;* a few other variants will be mentioned below.

As for combinations of the preterite and the past participle, the standard forms *drank-drunk* occur in all major areas, but they are not at all common. In N. Eng. about half the cultured informants (21/41) use this combination; outside the cultured group less than one tenth show these forms. In the M. A. S. the combination *drank-drunk* is used by about one third of the cultured informants, one fifth of Type II, and less than one twentieth of Type I. In the S. A. S. the standard forms strongly predominate in cultured speech, but show little frequency in the other types. Apparently in N. C. *drank-drunk* is making most progress in popular speech, being used by nearly one third of the Type II informants.

Among the very large number of informants who do not use the standard forms the prevalent practice is the leveling of preterite and past participle. Thus throughout N. Eng. the usual leveled form is *drank;* but here, and elsewhere, those who use *drunk* or *drinked* as preterite forms also use them as past participle forms.

The archaic past participle *drunken* /drʌŋkən/, in the combination *drank-drunken,* is used by 15 informants, scattered through all the major areas. Nine of these are cultured informants.

Drank-drinked occurs five times in N. Eng., 13 times in the M. A. S., and 11 times in the S. A. S. This combination occurs in several contiguous communities in n.e. Pa. and e. N. Y.; elsewhere it is in isolation.

The combination *drunk-drank* (the reversal of standard usage) occurs six times in N. Eng., four times in the M. A. S., and once in the S. A. S.

Other combinations that occur from once to six times each are *drank-drinken* /drɪŋkən/, *drunk-drinked,* *drinked-drank,* *drinked-drunk,* *drank-dranken* /dræŋkən/, *drinkened-drinken,* *dranken-drunk,* *drinken-drunk,* *dranked* /dræŋkt/ *-drinked,* *drunk-drinked* (Negro), *drinked-drinken* (Negro), and *drinked-drink,* in "Is you drink?" (Negro).[11]

A good many informants in N. Eng. give more than one form for the preterite or the past participle or both.

Drive (11)

The preterite and the past participle are recorded in the contexts "I (drove) in a nail" and "I have (driven) many nails."

As the preterite, *drove* /drov/ predominates in all major areas among all classes, its prevalence being limited only by the competing variants to be mentioned.

Driv /drɪv/ is used by 24/176 informants in n.e. N. Eng., usually alongside *drove.* Nearly all of these informants fall into Types IA (13) and IIA (eight). Two cultured informants (Conn. and N. H.), both over 70, use the form *driv.* Except for isolated instances (see Figure 8), *driv* occurs elsewhere principally in the coastal and mountain areas of the South and the South Midland. North Carolina shows the greatest frequency (36/143), all but five of the occurrences being in Type I. About one third of the Md., Va., and N. C. Negro informants use *driv.*

---

[11] Note that I have entered in Figure 7 only the occurrences of *drinked* as a preterite form; as a past participle form there are several additional occurrences, which do not appear on the map.

Druv /drʌv/ is not very frequent, occurring sporadically in n.e. N. Eng., s.e. Pa., and elsewhere as indicated on the map.

Droov /drʊv/ is used by three informants (N. J., Md. [Negro], and Va.).

Drive, uninflected, is used by five Southern Negroes, *drave* /drev/ by one, and *drived* /draivd/ by three Negro and three white informants.

As the past participle, the standard *driven* /drɪvən/ is used by the majority of informants throughout N. Eng. (except in Me., where most informants use *drove*). It is by far the most common form in the area around New York City, including n. N. J. and the lower Hudson Valley. Beginning in c. Pa. it becomes less and less frequent to the south and southwest until in N. C. about two thirds of the informants use some other form.

The most common deviation from the standard *drove-driven* is the leveled combination *drove-drove.* This is used by most Type I informants everywhere except for parts of s. and w. N. Eng. and the area around New York City. As for Type II informants, in most areas from one third to one half use the leveled forms; but in the entire area from the Merrimack to the Susquehanna the leveled forms are rather uncommon in this type of speech.

Other leveled forms of course also occur. Most informants who use *driv* and *druv* as the preterite also use them as past participle forms.

There are a few differentiated forms other than *drove-driven.* Ten informants, very widely scattered in the M. A. S. and the S. A. S., use *drove-droven* /drovən/; six, *driv-driven.* Other combinations that occur from one to four times each are *driv-drove, drove-driv, drove-druv, druv-driven, driv-druven* /drʌvən/, *droov* /drʊv/ *-driven, drived-drove* (Negro), *drive-driven* (Negro), and *drave-draven* /drevən/ (Negro). A number of informants who use these and the other combinations show more than one form for the preterite or the past participle or both.

Drown (96)

The past participle is recorded in the context "He was (drowned)."

The standard *drowned* /draund/ is almost universal in cultured speech everywhere, and it predominates in Type II speech (though not in Type I speech) in all major areas. Its frequency may be deduced from the prevalence of *drownded,* the only variant.

Drownded /draundəd/ is used by about one fourth of the N. Eng. informants, with the heaviest concentration in n. N. Eng. and in Conn. There is no striking difference in the noncultured types. Elsewhere in the Eastern States *drownded* is distinctly a Type I form, varying in frequency from one third (e. N. Y.) to nine tenths (N. C.). In Type II *drownded* is used by less than one tenth in e. N. Y., by about one fourth in Pa., Va., and N. C., and by slightly less than half in W. Va. About two thirds of the Southern Negro informants use this form.

Eat (48)

The preterite is recorded in the context "We (ate) at six o'clock," and the past participle in the context "How often have you (eaten) today?"

As the preterite, the form *ate* /et/ is very strongly favored by the cultured informants in all areas, and is fairly common in Type II speech. In Type I a more or less heavy majority use some other form except in s. N. Eng. and the area around New York City. The approximate extent of *ate* can be deduced from the frequency of the variants. In N. Eng. slightly over half the informants use a variant; these variants show little geographical concentration though they are least common in c. and w. Mass. In e. N. Y., N. J., and Pa. slightly less than half use a variant; everywhere else from half to nearly three fourths of the informants use some form other than *ate.*

The two variant preterite forms are *et* /ɛt/ and *eat* /it/. Figure 9 shows something of the geographical distribution of the two. The standard *ate* is completely disregarded in this map, the symbols indicating only the incidence of the popular forms *et* and *eat.*

The area of *et,* it will be seen, covers all of N. Eng. except Conn., and parts of N. Y. and n. Pa. *Et* is by no means confined to rustic usage; it is given by slightly over half the older informants (IA and IIA), but also by over one third of the younger (IB and IIB) groups. Five cultured informants in this area use *et.*

Eat, as is shown on the map, covers a large area in c. Pa., part of e. W. Va., most of Va. except the

Tidewater area, and nearly all of N. C. In this entire area the frequency of *eat* is very great, particularly as one moves southward. In the N. C. area of *eat*, over nine tenths of the Type I informants use it, as well as more than half of the Type II informants. No cultured informant anywhere uses the preterite *eat*.

In some rather large areas *et* and *eat* occur in about equal numbers. One of these areas takes in the valleys of the Kanawha and of the upper Ohio and its tributaries; another is a coastal area of some depth extending approximately from the James River to R. I. (excluding southern Delmarva). In both areas the occurrences are more frequent in the southern portions. In n. and w. N. Y., also, the two forms are found in about equal numbers, as they are in S. C. and e. Ga.

Since both *et* and *eat* are characteristically older forms and are apparently receding, it is difficult to state positively which of the two has lost favor more rapidly. However, there is some evidence, particularly in the eastern mixed areas, that *eat* is the more rustic and the least in favor. In eight communities in this area where two informants disagree, the more old-fashioned uses *eat* and the younger *et;* the opposite is true in six such communities. More than 10 cultured informants along the seaboard use *et,* and none use *eat.* These facts would indicate that in the past *et* has enjoyed more favor than *eat,* and that it is still a preferred form—even a prestige form—among many of the older cultured people of the coastal area.

Most informants who use *ate* in the preterite give *eaten* as the past participle. Among cultured informants *ate-eaten* strongly predominates everywhere, though it is by no means universal. About half the informants in N. Eng. use the standard combination *ate-eaten*, which has considerable currency even among Type I informants. Elsewhere the standard forms prevail among all classes only in a small area around New York City. In a somewhat larger area, a rather deep coastal strip extending roughly from Norfolk to Boston, *ate-eaten* is fairly common in Type II speech, though not always preponderant; and throughout N. C. nearly half the Type II informants use these forms. In that part of the Midland west of the Susquehanna, however, the combination *ate-eaten* is uncommon except in cultured speech.

Among the leveled combinations, *ate-ate* is the least common, being used by only eight informants in N. Eng. and 12 in the S. A. S. In the M. A. S. these forms are a little more common, particularly in Pa. (22/153) and W. Va. (9/100). Most of those who use *ate-ate* fall into Type II.

In the M. A. S. and the S. A. S. an overwhelming majority of those who use the preterite *et* also use this form as the past participle. In N. Eng. this same leveling is prevalent, but less universal; nearly one fourth of those who use the preterite *et* differentiate the preterite and the past participle, usually giving *eaten* for the latter. Cultured informants in all areas who use *et* invariably differentiate the preterite and the past participle.

Where the preterite *eat* is used, the past participle is almost invariably leveled.

Among the differentiated forms (other than *ate-eaten*), *et-eaten* shows considerable currency, especially in N. Eng., where more than one fifth of those who use the preterite *et* give the past participle as *eaten*. This combination is also current in the South, particularly in e. Va. and in S. C. A few cultured informants in N. Eng., New York City, Baltimore, Richmond, Charleston, and other points near the coast use this combination; no cultured informant who uses *et* gives any past participle form other than *eaten*.

The combination *et-eat* is extremely rare (10 occurrences) and is confined to Type I informants and Negroes, mostly in the Southern coastal areas.

Eat-eaten occurs in all major areas, though rather infrequently (23 occurrences). It is about equally common in Types I and II.

Ate-eat occurs only once in N. Eng., but it has some currency in the M. A. S. (38/411), showing most frequency in w. Pa., where it is used in several contiguous communities. This combination also occurs a few times in the S. A. S. It is most common among Type II informants.

There are also from six to eight occurrences of each of these combinations: *eat-ate, eat-et,* and *ate-et*.

In addition to all the combinations mentioned, a great many informants, especially in N. Eng., give more than one form for the preterite or the past participle or both. Many of the rarely occurring combinations, of course, probably do not indicate habitual differentiation of preterite and past participle, but merely hesitation between two or more current forms.

Fight (104)

The preterite is recorded in the context "They (fought) all the time." Data is available only for the M. A. S. and the S. A. S.

Fought /fɔt/ prevails in cultured speech everywhere; in the other types it is considerably limited in some areas, as will appear from the variants.

The form *fit* /fɪt/ (see Figure 10) occurs in the Hudson Valley, part of c. N. Y., and at some points in n. N. J. and n.e. Pa. In all of this area it is confined to Type I speech. South of the Pa.-Md. boundary there is another considerable area where the form occurs. Several instances may be noted along the upper Ohio and throughout n. W. Va. In the area south of the Kanawha, including s.w. Va. and w. N. C., this form is nearly universal in Type I and has considerable currency in Type II as well; in most communities in w. N. C. *fit* is used by both older and younger informants. *Fit* also occurs, though less universally, in n. c. N. C. and throughout the Piedmont area of Va., becoming extremely common again in a rather large area around Chesapeake Bay.

The preterite *fout* /faut/[12] occurs at several points along the Delaware and in nearly all the communities of s. N. J. There are a few scattered occurrences elsewhere in the M. A. S., as indicated on the map. In s.e. Va. south of the James and in a large area of e. N. C. and n.e. S. C. extending inland to or beyond the headwaters of the Peedee-Yadkin, *fout* occurs solidly in nearly all communities among Type I informants, and is used by about two thirds of the Type II informants as well. Both *fit* and *fout* occur rather often in w. S. C. and in Ga., outside the Charleston-Savannah Tidewater area.

It is hardly possible to determine which of the two forms *fit* and *fout* is the more rustic. In the South *fout* seems to be less restricted to Type I speech; however, informants who do not use *fit* or *fout* (and who comment on them) invariably classify both as "old," "old-fashioned," "used by Negroes," and so on.

Something over half the Negro informants in Md. and Va. use *fit;* all the N. C. Negroes use *fout.* Of Negro informants in S. C. and Ga., two use *fought,* one *fit,* two *fout,* and three the uninflected *fight.*

One cultured informant (Va.) uses *fit* along with *fought.*

Fit (27)

The preterite is recorded in the context "His coat (fitted) me."

Two preterite forms are current, the uninflected *fit* /fɪt/ and the inflected *fitted* /fɪtəd/. In N. Eng. the inflected form is strongly favored (being used by over three-fourths of all informants), with no particular distinction between the types, except that only three cultured informants use *fit*.[13]

In the M. A. S. and the S. A. S., on the other hand, *fitted* predominates only in e. N. C. It also occurs alongside *fit* (in about equal numbers) in N. Y., n. N. J., the Chesapeake Bay area, and parts of e. Pa. and w. N. C. Elsewhere in the East the uninflected *fit* is universal, or nearly so.

There is no clear evidence that one of these preterite forms is gaining at the expense of the other in the East as a whole. In communities of divided usage the more modern informant uses the uninflected form about as often as the more old-fashioned informant does. Cultured usage corresponds to popular usage in the treatment of this verb; i.e., in areas where one form predominates in popular speech, it also predominates in cultured speech. In the M. A. S. about two thirds of the cultured informants use *fit;* in the S. A. S. a little over half use this form.

Freeze (7)

The preterite is recorded in the context "The lake (froze) over last night."

Froze is with rare exceptions the only form used in N. Eng. and the M. A. S. (though many N. Eng. informants choose the phrase "skum /skʌm/ over," *skum* apparently being the preterite of *skim*). As will be seen from Figure 11, the variant forms belong characteristically and almost exclusively to

---

[12] The /au/ in this form is not to be confused with the diphthongized /ɔ/ ([ɒɔ], and so on) that occurs in the South. The two are kept distinct in Southern speech; and in the cases of *fout* that I have indicated, the /au/ phonemes are used, not the /ɔ/.

[13] Note that although *fit* and *knit* are both presented on Map 647 of the *Linguistic Atlas of New England* (ed. Hans Kurath and Bernard Bloch; 3 vols. in 6 parts; Providence, R. I.: Brown Univ., 1939–43), the distribution of forms for the two verbs is quite different in N. Eng.

the South, occurring with greatest frequency in the coastal areas.

Freezed /frizd/ is a fairly common variant, being used by something over one tenth of the informants in Va. and N. C. (it is much less commonly recorded in S. C.). All but two who use this form are Type I informants; about one fourth of the Va., N. C., and S. C. Negro informants use it.

Frozed /frozd/ is about as common as *freezed*, and is also almost entirely confined to Type I informants. It occurs most commonly in the Tidewater areas, though it extends inland some distance, especially in N. C. One Negro informant uses this form.

Friz /frɪz/ occurs only rarely, and then in isolation except for two contiguous communities in Anson and Cabarrus counties in N. C. All together, there are only nine occurrences of *friz*, divided among informants in N. H., Pa., Md., Va., N. C., and S. C. One of these is a N. C. Negro.

Frez /frɛz/ occurs among eight Type I informants in e. Va. and n. c. N. C. It is also used by more than one third of the Md., Va., and N. C. Negro informants.

Other preterite forms used by one or two informants each are: *frozen* /frozən/ (N. C. and S. C.), *freezen* /frizən/ (Va. and N. C.), and *frazed* /frezd/ (Md., S. C. [Negro]).

All of the variant preterite forms noted are distinctly older forms and are no doubt receding rapidly.

Give (102)

The preterite is recorded in the context "That's the one you (gave) me."

Gave /gev/ is nearly universal in cultured speech and predominates in Type II speech in all areas, being limited in that type by the variants to be mentioned.

The uninflected *give* /gɪv/ occurs in nearly two thirds of the communities investigated in N. Eng.,[14] with no particular concentration except that this form is uncommon in R. I. and c. Mass. In something over a third of these communities *give* is used by the more modern informant (or by both older and younger informants); in others only the more old-fashioned informant uses it. Around New

---

[14] The assimilated forms /ˈgɪmmi/ and /ˈgɪmi/ are regarded as occurrences of *give*.

York City *give* hardly occurs at all; it is not very common in n. N. J., and less than half the Type I informants in e. N. Y. use it. Elsewhere in the East *give* is used by something like from two thirds (Pa.) to over nine tenths (Va. and N. C.) of Type I. In Type II the frequency is considerably less, varying from about one fourth (Pa.) to about two fifths (W. Va.). Three cultured informants in N. Eng. and one in Pa. use *give*.

Sixteen N. Eng. informants, mostly in N. H. and Me., and two Southern informants use the form *gin* /gɪn/; nearly all of them also use *give* or *gave* or both. The form *gin* is characteristically an older (IA and IIA) form. Two Southern informants state that *gin* is "used by Negroes," yet none of the Negro informants offer that form (*give* being almost universal among them). One Negro, however, uses the weak form *gived* /gɪvd/.

Grow (65)

The preterite and the past participle are recorded in N. Eng. in the contexts "Bob (grew) a lot in one year" and "You've (grown) big." In the M. A. S. and the S. A. S. only the preterite is recorded.

The preterite *grew* /gru/ is universal in cultured speech. It predominates heavily among all classes throughout s. N. Eng., in the area around New York City (including n. N. J. and the lower Hudson Valley), and in most of the larger cities of the East. Elsewhere it prevails in Type II speech, but in most areas not in Type I speech.

The preterite *growed* /grod/ occurs in very scattered fashion in s. and w. N. Eng., while in the northeast it shows considerable frequency, though many who use it also use *grew*. It is used by about three fourths of Type IA informants in n.e. N. Eng. and by from one fourth to one third of the other noncultured informants. Elsewhere *growed* occurs in Type I speech with a frequency varying from about one third (e. N. Y. and N. J.) to well over nine tenths (N. C.). In Type II it is rare in N. Y., N. J., and Del.; elsewhere it is used by from one fourth to nearly one half of this group.

In N. Eng. the predominant past participle form is *grown* /gron/. This is used by nearly all who give *grew* as the preterite and by almost half of those who use the preterite *growed*. The combination *grew-growed* occurs in seven scattered communities.

Hang (85)

The past participle is recorded in the context "The murderer was (hanged)."

The form *hung* /hʌŋ/ predominates in all areas and among all types.

In N. Eng. about one fourth of the informants give the form *hanged* /hæŋd/, more often than not alongside *hung*. There is no clear distinction between the age groups, but *hanged* is slightly more common in the educated types (IIIA and IIIB) than in Types I and II. Of the cultured informants, nine use only *hanged*, six others use both *hanged* and *hung*.

In the M. A. S. *hanged* is used by about one sixth of the Type I informants and by about one third each of the Type II and the cultured informants.

In the S. A. S. *hanged* is rare (10 occurrences) in Type I and is used by a little less than one third of the Type II and the cultured informants.

Hear (12)

The past participle is recorded in the two contexts "I have (heard) it" and "I have (heard) tell."

Very few variants occur in N. Eng., there being but two instances of *heered* /hird/, eight of *heern* /hirn/, and four of *hearn* /hɜn/. The standard *heard* /hɜd/ prevails throughout this area, as it does in N. Y., most of N. J., and most of the eastern half of Pa. From c. Pa. to the southwest the form *heered* /hird/ becomes increasingly common among informants of Type I. A related form /hjɜd/, which obviously results from a shift of stress to the second element of the [iɚ]-type diphthong, begins to be recorded in n. W. Va. and becomes more and more frequent to the south and southwest; in the mountain areas south of the Kanawha it is almost the only variant recorded. A number of Type II informants in this area use the /hird/-/hjɜd/ variety, but nowhere is it dominant in that type.

Heern /hirn/ or /hjɜn/ shows a typical Southern distribution (see Figure 12). It covers the southern half of Delmarva and the remainder of the Tidewater area of the South; in Va. it extends inland to the Blue Ridge and in N. C. no farther than

the lower Piedmont, except that in n.w. N. C. it reaches westward to the headwaters of the New River (see map). It is current but less frequent in e. S. C. Three communities in c. W. Va. also show this form. In the idiomatic "heard tell," as is typical of archaisms, *heern* is considerably more frequent than in "heard it."[15] Of the informants who use *heern*, well over three fourths fall into Type I. Throughout the South and the South Midland almost all informants of this type use either *heered* or *heern*. No cultured informant uses either form.

Heat (50)

Data on this verb is very limited, since the phrase recorded is "warmed over," in which only a small proportion of the informants substitute the verb *heat* for *warm*.

The past participle (adjective) form *het* /hɛt/ ("het up" or "het over") is quite common in n.e. N. Eng., where about one fourth of the informants offer it in this context. In many communities the more modern as well as the more old-fashioned informant gives this form, sometimes alongside *warmed* or *heated*.

Elsewhere in the Eastern States only a sprinkling of informants use *het* in this context (18 in the M. A. S., 29 in the S. A. S.), with no geographical concentration. Three cultured informants in the M. A. S. give *het*.

Help (49, 58)

The preterite and the past participle are recorded in the contexts "I (helped) myself" and "He might have (helped) me." Data is not available for N. Eng.

Helped /hɛlpt/ is universal on all levels throughout the M. A. S. (except for a portion of s. W. Va.), and in cultured speech everywhere.

The form *holp* /hop/, used as both preterite and past participle, shows a striking geographical concentration (see Figure 13). Its northern boundary forms an arc beginning in c. Del., running a little to the north of Baltimore, and curving back to the southward into n. Va. Except for one point in Warren County, *holp* does not extend beyond the Blue Ridge until the vicinity of Roanoke, to the west of which it extends into s.w. Va. and a portion

---

[15] E.g., in Va. 38 informants use "heern tell," 18 use "heern it"; in N. C. 54 use "heern tell," 35 use "heern it."

of s. W. Va. Within the area indicated, *holp* occurs in almost every community (a little less commonly in S. C. and Ga.); outside this area it does not occur at all, even in isolation. With very few exceptions, those who use *holp* as the preterite also use it as the past participle, and vice versa. Nearly all the Type I informants give *holp* as either the preterite or the past participle or both.

There is only one occurrence of *holped* /hopt/, i.e., in Baltimore County, Md., the northernmost point of the *holp* area.

Kneel (96)

The preterite is recorded in the context "She (knelt) down." *Knelt* /nɛlt/ is the dominant form in all major areas, and is heavily favored by cultured informants.

Kneeled /nild/ is used by about one third of the N. Eng. informants, with no sharp distinction between the age and the education groups. In about three fifths of the communities of divided usage *kneeled* is given by the more old-fashioned informant. Eight cultured informants give only *kneeled*, two others give *kneeled* alongside *knelt*.

In the M. A. S. something less than one fourth of the informants use *kneeled*, this form being slightly more common in Type I than in Type II and least common (used by about one eighth) in the cultured group.

In the S. A. S. something like two fifths of the informants use *kneeled*. In Va. it is about equally common in Types I and II; in Md. and N. C. it is considerably more common in Type I. Six cultured informants in Va. and one in Del. use *kneeled;* in Md. and N. C. this form is not recorded in cultured speech.

McDavid frequently records *kneel* (without /d/) before *down;* Lowman rarely does so.

Two informants (W. Va. and N. C.) give *kneed* /nid/; one (Negro) uses *kneened* /nind/.

Knit (27)

In N. Eng., only, the preterite is recorded in the context "They (knitted) sweaters for the soldiers." The uninflected *knit* /nɪt/ is dominant throughout N. Eng., being used by well over three fourths of all informants. In n.e. N. Eng. it is practically universal, there being only occasional exceptions.

The inflected form *knitted* /nɪtəd/ is found most frequently in Mass., Conn., and Vt. This is clearly a newer form than *knit;* in nearly all (27/33) communities of divided usage *knitted* is the form given by the more modern informant.

Cultured informants are about equally divided between the two forms.

Know (101)

The preterite is recorded in the context "I just (knew) it." This item was not on the N. Eng. work sheets, but was recorded throughout the M. A. S. and the S. A. S.

Knew /nju/ or /nu/ is universal in cultured speech and almost so in Type II speech north and east of the Susquehanna. Its currency elsewhere may be seen from an account of the variants.

The weak preterite *knowed* /nod/ is used in all major areas, but in e. N. Y., N. J., and e. Pa. it is a rustic and rather uncommon form (less than one sixth of Type I informants use it). From c. Pa. to the south and southwest, *knowed* becomes more and more common, being used by more than nine tenths of the Type I informants in Va. and N. C. and by almost as many in S. C. and Ga. In the M. A. S. and in Del. and Md. not a great many Type II informants use this form, but in Va. about half use it, and in N. C. about two thirds do so.

Of the 16 Negro informants who give a response in Md., Va., and N. C., 14 give *knowed* and two the uninflected *know* /no/.

Known /non/ is used as a preterite by one Md. informant.

Learn (101)

In the item "Who (taught) you that?" the verb *learn* is substituted by about half the N. Eng. informants, and by from half to three fourths of the informants in the other areas.

Two preterite forms are current, *learned* (usually /lɜndʒə/) and *learnt* (usually /lɜntʃə/).[16] In all areas *learnt* predominates rather markedly (being used by two thirds of the informants); in some sections (e.g., most of Va.) *learned* hardly occurs at all. In the East as a whole, however, *learned* is gaining rapidly over *learnt;* in more than four fifths

---

[16] The types /lɑrnd/ and /lɑrnt/ are occasionally found in n.e. N. Eng. and also occur in parts of the S. A. S., particularly N. C. All informants in the S. A. S. who use /ɑr/ form the preterite with the /-t/ affix, /lɑrnt/.

of the communities of divided usage *learned* is given by the more modern informant, *learnt* by the more old-fashioned.

Lie (96–97)

The present infinitive and the preterite are recorded in the contexts "I'm going to (lie) down" and "He (lay) in bed all day."

In general, the present form *lie* /lai/ predominates in all major areas, being used by from three fifths to two thirds of all informants, without any significant geographical distribution. The alternate form *lay* /le/ is slightly more common among Type I informants (about half of whom use it) than among Type II. On the whole, however, *lay* seems characteristic of certain communities, rather than of certain more old-fashioned informants within those communities. Only a scattering of cultured informants give the present form *lay*, and then usually alongside *lie*.

The preterite forms can best be surveyed in terms of their corresponding present forms. The combination *lie : lay* is of very limited occurrence. In n. N. Eng. and in e. N. Eng. (except for a few points in R. I. and e. Conn.) this combination is quite rare outside of cultured speech, and only about half the cultured informants in these areas use it. In s.w. N. Eng. *lie : lay* is universal in cultured usage and occurs among a fair number of noncultured informants as well.

In the entire M. A. S. *lie : lay* is uncommon among noncultured informants (being used by less than one twelfth of the group), and is confined to about one third of the cultured group.

In the S. A. S. *lie : lay* is rare in Del., Md., and the Piedmont area of Va., but becomes much more common (and might even be called the dominant popular usage) on the Eastern Shore of Va. and throughout most of N. C. and part of S. C. A little less than half the cultured informants in the S. A. S. use the *lie : lay* combination.

A much more common practice is the combination of the present *lie* with the preterite *laid* /led/ ("going to lie down" : "laid in bed"). Of those who use the present *lie*, a considerable majority (two thirds in N. Eng., four fifths in the M. A. S.) combine it with the preterite *laid*. Only in N. C. and on the Eastern Shore of Va. is this combination somewhat uncommon. In e. N. Eng. about half

the cultured informants give *lie : laid;* in the M. A. S. and the S. A. S. something more than half do so.

Some eight informants in N. Eng. and five in other areas use the combination *lie : lied* /laid/. This feature shows no concentration and may represent a groping for a "correct" form rather than habitual usage.

Of those who use the present *lay*, a heavy majority in most areas form the preterite as *laid*. An exception may be found in N. C., where a considerable number use the leveled present and preterite *lay : lay*. This leveling also occurs in a very scattered way in N. Eng. and parts of Pa.

Nearly all Negro informants use the forms *lay : laid;* one (S. C.), however, uses the leveled forms *lie : lie*.

In summary, we may say that as a present form *lie* is predominant in all areas, and that as the preterite of both *lie* and *lay*, *laid* is very heavily predominant everywhere except in the areas of the S. A. S. mentioned above where *lay* predominates as preterite.

Might (58)

This form is recorded only in the M. A. S. and the S. A. S. in the contexts "He (might) have helped me" and "I (might) be able."

The archaic *mought* /maut/ occurs in the S. A. S. in a distribution very similar to that of *holp* (see above). It extends into the Shenandoah Valley at three points, however, and there are occurrences in the eastern portion of W. Va. and even in w. Md. It is recorded in three scattered communities in c. and n. N. J. (see Figure 14). *Mought* is primarily a rustic form, being used by more than half the Type I informants in Va. and N. C. but by less than one sixth the Type II informants.

"Might be able" usually appears as "might could" in the South; only about two thirds as many informants use *mought* in this phrase as use it in "might have helped."

Plead (23)

In N. Eng., only, the preterite is recorded in the context "He (pleaded) guilty."

The dominant preterite form is *pled* /plɛd/, which is used by nearly three fourths of all informants in N. Eng., without any geographical or social concentration. The alternate form *pleaded* /plidəd/ is a little more common in n. Me. and New Brunswick than elsewhere, but occurs in all major areas of N. Eng. Of the cultured informants, 26 give *pled*, eight give *pleaded*, and two give both forms.

Ride (34)

The past participle is recorded in the context "I have never (ridden) a horse."

Ridden /rɪdən/ is universal in cultivated speech, and it predominates in popular usage in certain areas, being used by a majority of the Type II informants throughout N. Eng. (except Me.), N. Y., and N. J. It has some currency in Type II usage everywhere, though it is considerably limited by *rode* throughout the Midland and the South. *Ridden* prevails in Type I usage only in s. N. Eng., n. N. J., and the lower Hudson Valley, though many of the informants in this group in n.e. N. Eng. know and use this form alongside a variant.

Rode /rod/, which in nearly all occurrences would indicate leveling of the preterite and the past participle, predominates rather heavily in n.e. N. Eng. among the older informants (IA and IIA) and is used by about half the younger ones (IB and IIB) as well. In this area many of those who use *rode* also know and use *ridden*. In s. and w. N. Eng. *rode* is more scattered and more characteristic of older informants.

Except for n. N. J. and the lower Hudson Valley, where *rode* is rather infrequent, this form predominates very strongly in Type I throughout the M. A. S. and the S. A. S.; and it is also used by from one half to two thirds of the Type II informants.

The archaic *rid* /rɪd/ (see Figure 15) occurs in a scattered way in n.e. N. Eng., being confined to informants of Types IA and IIA, most of whom also use *rode* or *ridden* or both. Elsewhere in the East *rid* is extremely rare until one reaches the coastal and mountain areas of the South and the South Midland. It has its greatest frequency in N. C., where it is used by about one third of the Type I informants (it hardly occurs among those of Type II). Three Southern Negroes use *rid;* almost all the others give *rode*. One informant in Georgetown, S. C., uses *ride* as a participle.

Ring (11)

In N. Eng., only, the preterite is recorded in the context "Who (rang) the bell?"

The two preterite forms *rang* /ræŋ/ and *rung* /rʌŋ/ occur with about equal frequency in s. N. Eng. *Rung* is clearly the more old-fashioned form, although in some communities it is prevalent among modern informants as well. North and east of the Merrimack *rung* is very heavily predominant in all types of speech; in most of Me. and in New Brunswick *rang* is not recorded at all.

Six cultured informants in N. Eng. use only the form *rung;* two others give *rung* alongside *rang*.

Rise (3)

Only the preterite is recorded, in the context "The sun (rose) at six"; however, the past participle or adjective form also occurs in N. Eng., in the phrase "riz bread."

The standard preterite form *rose* /roz/ prevails throughout N. Eng., N. Y., N. J., and Pa., and is not uncommon among younger informants everywhere. Its exact currency cannot be determined, since many informants choose other words, such as *come up* or (particularly in the South Midland) *raise*.

Riz /rɪz/ occurs with some frequency in n.e. N. Eng. (see Figure 16), usually alongside *rose*. There are 37/176 occurrences of it in this area, 35 of which come from Types IA (20) and IIA (15); age seems more significant here than lack of education, though no cultured informant uses this form. "Riz bread" has somewhat more currency (56 occurrences) in n.e. N. Eng.; moreover, it is used by a few informants in e. Mass., Nantucket, and Martha's Vineyard who do not say "the sun riz." One cultured informant (N. H.) uses "riz bread." In s. N. Eng. and throughout the whole of the M. A. S. *riz* occurs only in a very scattered way (see Figure 16), and almost entirely among Type I informants. In the S. A. S., however, it is the dominant form in Type I (110/189); it has a little currency in Type II (15/145); and most (8/14) Va. and N. C. Negro informants use it.

Rised /raizd/ occurs principally in W. Va. and adjoining parts of Va. and O.; its frequency is not great (12/100 in W. Va.), and its use is about equally divided between Types I and II.

Rise /raiz/, the uninflected preterite form, is with one exception confined to Va., N. C., and S. C. Negroes, about one fourth of whom use it.

Raised /rezd/ (almost certainly with a present form *raise* /rez/) is rare in this context in N. Eng. and the S. A. S., but is scattered through the M. A. S., reaching its greatest frequency in W. Va. (33/100). About one third of those who use *raised* are Type II informants.

Run (102)

The preterite is recorded in the context "He (ran)."

The preterite *ran* /ræn/ predominates rather strongly in e. N. Y. and n. N. J.; it occurs in about half the communities of s. N. Eng. and Pa. Elsewhere it is more or less sharply limited by the form *run*.

Run /rʌn/ predominates among the more old-fashioned informants in s. N. Eng. and among all the noncultured types in n. N. Eng. In fact, north and east of the Merrimack *ran* hardly occurs at all outside of cultivated speech. In e. N. Y. and n. N. J. *run* is not very common, being confined to about one fourth of the Type I informants. In the remainder of the M. A. S., as in Del. and Md., this form is used by from two thirds (Pa.) to over nine tenths (W. Va.) of Type I informants and by from one third (Pa.) to one half (W. Va. and Md.) of Type II. In Va. and N. C. *run* is used by nearly all the informants of both Type I and Type II; in S. C. and Ga. the percentage is not quite so high. In general, south of the Potomac, as well as northeast of the Merrimack, the form *ran* does not normally occur except in cultured speech. About one fourth of the cultured informants in N. Eng. use the preterite *run,* but in the M. A. S. and the S. A. S. this form occurs only twice in this type of speech.

See (102)

The preterite is recorded in the context "He (saw) me."

The standard *saw* /sɔ/ is practically universal in cultured speech; in the other types it is universally recorded only in c. Mass. and in a small area around New York City. Elsewhere the variant forms occur in from most to nearly all communities.

The uninflected preterite *see* /si/ (see Figure 17) is by far the most common variant form in N. Eng.

(preponderating by more than five to one over other variants). In s. N. Eng. this is clearly an older form; in n. and n.e. N. Eng. it is quite current in all the noncultured groups, being used by from half of Type IIB informants to more than four fifths of Type IA. *See* also prevails in N. Y. and the northernmost edge of Pa., mostly (three fourths) in Type I speech. It predominates over other variants in the Piedmont area of Va. and part of the Tidewater area, as well as in parts of n.e. N. C. In these areas it is almost exclusively a Type I form.

The form *seen* /sin/ occurs only in a scattered way in the northern areas mentioned above—most commonly in n. and w. N. Y. It strongly predominates in the Midland area—including most of N. J., the southern three fourths of Pa., W. Va. (except a small southern portion), most of Del. and Md., part of n. and w. Va., some portions of N. C., and all of S. C. and e. Ga. Throughout this territory *seen* is used by from two thirds (Pa.) to nearly all (W. Va.) of the Type I informants, as well as by from half (Pa.) to two thirds (W. Va.) of the Type II. Only in the Shenandoah Valley and adjoining areas of Va. is *seen* definitely a Type I form.

The weak preterite *seed* /sid/ occurs once in N. Eng.; otherwise there are no occurrences north of the Pa.-Md. boundary. In the mountain areas south of the Kanawha this form becomes quite common, being used by most Type I informants as well as by a few of Type II. *Seed* extends more or less all across N. C., in some areas being the only preterite form in use other than *saw. Seed* also occurs in a rather scattered way in S. C. and e. Ga.

No cultured informant uses *see* or *seed; seen* occurs twice in this type (Pa. and W. Va.).

Seed is the most common form among Southern Negroes, though *seen* and *see* also occur.

Shrink (27)

The preterite is recorded in the context "The collar (shrank)." In N. Eng., only, the past participle is also recorded, in the context "It has (shrunk)." The records of *shrink* are not complete, since in the South and the South Midland a very large number of informants choose the phrase *draw up* (preterite *drawed* or *drew*).

Among the users of the verb *shrink*, the preterite

shrunk /ʃrʌŋk/ or often /srʌŋk/ strongly predominates among all types in all areas. Considerably less than one eighth of the informants in N. Eng., and not many more in any area, use any other preterite form. It is rather strongly favored by cultured informants (something over half in N. Eng. and at least three fourths in the M. A. S. and the S. A. S. use it)—though a good many in this group use *shrunk* and *shrank* interchangeably.

Shrank /ʃræŋk/ or /sræŋk/ is scattered throughout the East, though it is almost unknown in the South. It appears on all levels, but especially the cultured level, being used by about one fourth of the cultured informants in N. Eng. and the M. A. S., and by something less than one eighth in the S. A. S.

Shrinked /ʃrɪŋkt/ is extremely rare and scattered, showing nothing like concentration except in the Susquehanna Valley and adjoining areas, where 11 informants use it.

Swunk /swʌŋk/ occurs twice in N. Eng., twice in the M. A. S., and 11 times in the S. A. S.

Swinked /swɪŋkt/ is used by five Southern informants (three Negro), *swink* /swɪŋk/ by one (Negro), *shrink* /ʃrɪŋk/ by six (three Negro), *shranked* /ʃræŋkt/ by one (N. J.), and *strinked* /strɪŋkt/ by one (N. J.).

As the past participle (recorded in N. Eng. only), six informants use *shrank*, of whom four use *shrunk* as the preterite.

A sizable minority in N. Eng. (64/413) use *shrunken* /ʃrʌŋkən/ as a past participle in this context. Most of these are in w. N. Eng., and a fair number (10) are cultured informants.

Shrinked is used as the past participle by two informants, and *swunk* by two.

Sit (49)

The present imperative and the preterite are recorded in the contexts "(Sit) down" and "I (sat) down." In N. Eng. the record of the present forms is not complete, since fieldworkers often recorded phrases containing other verbs than *sit*.

Two present forms (or separate verbs) are current, *sit* /sɪt/ and *set* /sɛt/. *Sit* predominates among all types in New York City, n. N. J., the lower Hudson Valley, and Pa. east of the Susquehanna. Elsewhere in Pa. and N. Y. the forms are about equally distributed. In the entire area to the south of Pa., outside of the larger cities, *sit* is rather uncommon except in cultured speech.

Of the informants who use the present *sit*, those in the coastal areas strongly prefer the preterite *sat* /sæt/. Farther inland, particularly in c. and w. Pa. and in W. Va., there is a tendency to use the leveled forms *sit* : *sit*. More than a few use the combination *sit* : *set*, chiefly in c. and w. Pa. and W. Va., and three or four in N. Y. and n.e. Pa. use *sit* : *sot* /sɑt/.

Among informants who use the present *set*, by far the most common preterite throughout the M. A. S. is the leveled form *set*. This is also true in the S. A. S. except in the areas where *sot* predominates (see below). However, another combination, *set* : *sat*, is occasionally found throughout the East, being most common in e. Va., where 14 informants use it. A combination that is far from uncommon in the S. A. S. is *set* : *sot*. Almost all the informants in the East who give *sot* as the preterite (see Figure 18) use *set* as the present.

Something of the frequency of the preterite forms has appeared in the account of the various combinations. Figure 18 shows the approximate geographical distribution of the variant preterites *sit* and *sot*. *Sit*, it will be observed, shows tendencies toward concentration in w. N. Eng. and parts of Pa. and W. Va., but is not very common in areas where *sot* prevails. *Sit* is about equally common in Types I and II. *Sot*, on the other hand, is distinctly an archaism, and, though it occurs in nearly all the major areas, it is most common in the more conservative areas—n.e. N. Eng., the South, and parts of the South Midland (including nearly all of N. C.). Of the 30 occurrences of *sot* in N. Eng., 25 are in the older types (IA and IIA); in the M. A. S. and the S. A. S. more than nine tenths of the occurrences are in Type I.

Spoil (46)

The past participle (adjective) form is recorded in the context "The meat is (spoiled)."

The only two forms in use in the East are *spoiled* /spɔild/ and *spoilt* /spɔilt/ (with the variants /spaild/ and /spailt/).[17]

---

[17] The use of /ai/ rather than /ɔi/ in *spoil*, as well as in *boil* (see above, p. 6), is fairly common in the rustic speech of n. N. Eng. and of parts of the South and the South Midland.

In N. Eng. and N. Y. the form with /d/ predominates strongly (being used by about three fourths of the informants), with the /t/ form characteristic of (but not confined to) old-fashioned speech. In most other areas of the East the /t/ form is more common, being used by about three fourths of Type I and about half of Type II.

Spoilt has some currency in cultured speech, though nowhere does it predominate. In N. Eng. about one fourth of the cultured informants use this form, in the M. A. S. about one eighth, in the S. A. S. over one third.

Steal (100)

Data on this verb is very incomplete, since in the item "Who (swiped) my pencil?" the main object was to record synonyms for *steal*. In the S. A. S., however, most informants use *steal* in this context.

The preterite form *stole* is very heavily predominant in the records gathered by Lowman; only a scattering of informants give the form *stoled* /stold/ before *my*, and three fourths of these are in Type I. However, in this phrase the /d/ would be expected to assimilate to the following consonant. In S. C. and Ga. McDavid often recorded this verb before *it*, and *stoled* occurred a rather large number of times. We might reasonably conjecture that *stoled* would have been of fairly common occurrence if recorded before a vowel.

One S. C. informant uses *stealed* /stild/, and one Va. Negro gives the uninflected *steal* /stil/.

Sweat (77)

The preterite is recorded in the context "He (sweated) hard." A few informants avoid using this verb, presumably because of its unpleasant connotation to them.

The uninflected *sweat* /swɛt/ is practically universal throughout the entire Northern area (N. Eng., N. Y., n. N. J., and the northern half of Pa.), where less than one out of 20 informants use the alternate form *sweated*.

Beginning in c. Pa., the inflected form *sweated* /swɛtəd/ becomes increasingly frequent as one moves southward. It predominates in Md. (two thirds use it) and N. C. (four fifths use it), whereas in Va. and S. C. *sweat* and *sweated* are about equally common.

There is no noticeable difference between Types I and II in the choice of forms, nor does cultured usage show any perceptible variation from popular usage. In N. Eng. *sweated* is used by one eighth of the cultured informants, in the M. A. S. by one third, in the S. A. S. by two thirds.

Swell (77)

The preterite is recorded in the context "My hand (swelled) up," and the past participle (or adjective) in the context "It is (swollen)."

The preterite form *swelled* /swɛld/ is strongly predominant in all areas among all classes; the variants, as will be seen, occur among only a small fraction of the informants.

The preterite *swole* /swol/ occurs a few times (20) in N. Eng., being more common in the Plymouth and Cape Cod areas than elsewhere. It is most common among the older groups, but not entirely confined to them. Elsewhere in the East there are scattered occurrences of *swole,* and in a few areas it shows some concentration. It occurs in about half the communities of e. S. C. (including Charleston); it is found in several contiguous communities (including Richmond) along the lower James Valley; and three informants in New York City use it.

There are about 20 occurrences of *swoled* /swold/, widely scattered through all the major areas.

Swollen /swolən/ (as preterite) shows some 25 occurrences, nearly all in the S. A. S.; it indicates some tendency to concentration in the southern Piedmont of Va.

It is striking that many informants who use the preterites *swole, swoled,* and *swollen* in Va., N. C., and S. C. characterize *swelled* as "old," "old-fashioned," "used as a child," and so on. The three New York City informants who use *swole* are among the youngest in the noncultured types. It seems that for some reason the variants mentioned have been spreading at the expense of *swelled* in fairly recent times.

The uninflected *swell* /swɛl/ is used by about 12 informants, four of them Negroes. Other forms that occur from once to seven times each are *swollened* /swolənd/, *swellened* /swɛlənd/, *swone* /swon/, *swull* /swʌl/, *swulled* /swʌld/ or /swʊld/, and *swelt* /swɛlt/.

Among the combinations of preterite and past participle (or adjective), *swelled-swollen* is almost universal in cultured speech everywhere. It predominates among all types in s. N. Eng. and elsewhere is fairly common in Type II, being used by something like from one third (N. C.) to two thirds (N. Y.) of this group. In Type I it is rather narrowly limited by the variants to be mentioned.

The leveled forms *swelled-swelled* predominate (99/176) in n.e. N. Eng. among both older and younger groups, though many informants also know and use the alternate past participle form *swollen*. In s. and w. N. Eng. the leveled forms are not very common. Elsewhere in the Eastern States the leveled *swelled-swelled* predominates among Type I informants except in e. N. Y. and N. J., where about one third of this type show leveling. From Pa. to N. C. about half to three fourths of Type I give the leveled forms. In Type II this leveling occurs in from one fifth (e. N. Y.) to one half (N. C. and W. Va.) of the informants.

Other combinations of preterite and past participle occur in more or less scattered fashion. Nearly all of those who use *swole* as the preterite (see above) give the past participle as *swollen;* only three use the leveled *swole-swole*, and two use *swole-swelled*.

All who use the preterite *swollen* use this form as the past participle as well.

The combination *swelled-swullen* /swʌlən/ shows a fairly high frequency in the Hudson Valley, n. N. J., s.e. Pa., and along the upper tributaries of the Ohio in w. Pa. In the same areas there are a few instances of *swole-swullen, swullen-swullen, swoled-swullen*, and *swull* /swʌl/ *-swullen*.

Other combinations that occur more or less in isolation are *swelled-swellen, swelled-swellened, swulled* /swʊld/ *-swollen, swelled-swolden* /swoldən/, and *swelled-swole*.

Swim (95)

The preterite is recorded in the context "I (swam) across."

Swam /swæm/ is universal in cultured speech everywhere. It predominates in all types throughout most of s. N. Eng., N. Y., and n. N. J., and is favored in Type II speech nearly everywhere, with limitations that will be indicated.

Swum /swʌm/ predominates in n.e. N. Eng., particularly among the older types. In s. N. Eng. about half the older informants use it, and only a scattering of the younger. In e. N. Y. and n. N. J. less than one fourth of the older group use this form, and it hardly occurs at all in Type II. Elsewhere in the M. A. S. and in the S. A. S. *swum* predominates in Type I speech, its frequency varying from slightly over half (Pa.) to nearly nine tenths (N. C.). In Type II its occurrence is much more limited, varying from less than one sixth (Pa.) to nearly half (W. Va. and N. C.). *Swum* is used by seven cultured informants, three of whom give it alongside *swam*.

What is particularly striking is the extent to which *swum* is being replaced by *swam*. In N. Eng. I count 57 communities where usage is clearly divided between the two forms; in 48 of these the more old-fashioned informant uses *swum,* the more modern *swam*. In the M. A. S. the change is toward *swam* in 66 out of 78 such communities; in the S. A. S., in 70 out of 75.[18]

There are two occurrences of *swimmed* /swɪmd/ in N. Eng., four in the M. A. S., and over 35 in the S. A. S. Of the S. A. S. occurrences, 17 are within the eastern two thirds of N. C.

The uninflected *swim* /swɪm/ is used by only two informants in the M. A. S.; in the S. A. S. about 40 informants use it, most of the occurrences being in S. C. and Ga.

Take (20, 76–77)

The preterite is recorded in the context "Who (took) my knife?," the past participle in the contexts "He (got = was taken) sick" and "Haven't you (taken) your medicine yet?"

The standard preterite *took* /tʊk/ is practically universal in cultured speech, and among all classes throughout N. Eng. and the M. A. S. as far south as the Pa.-Md. boundary. South of this line *took* is dominant in Type II speech and is not uncommon in Type I speech, with the limitations to be noted.

The preterite *tuck* /tʌk/ shows six scattered occurrences in N. Eng., Pa., and N. J. (see Figure 19). In Delmarva, the Tidewater area of Virginia, and nearly all of N. C. it becomes fairly common (being used by more than half of Type I in N. C.). It

---

[18] This figure does not include the McDavid records, which, however, present essentially the same picture.

also occurs with some regularity in s.w. Va. and throughout W. Va., and is found in a scattered way in S. C. and Ga. In Va. this form occurs on nearly all sides of the Piedmont area, but is missing from the Piedmont itself. *Tuck* is primarily a Type I form, over seven eighths of its occurrences being in this group.

The preterite *taken* /tekən/ is also confined to the South and the South Midland, where it occurs rather commonly in Md. and W. Va., less commonly in Va., N. C., and S. C. This form is demonstrably newer than *tuck*. Although in the Piedmont area of Va. (where *tuck* does not occur) most (19/25) of the occurrences of *taken* are in Type I, elsewhere about half or more are in Type II. In 16 out of 21 communities where both forms occur the more old-fashioned informant gives *tuck* and the more modern, *taken*.

There are 26 instances of the preterite *takened* /tekənd/, most of which are in Delmarva, the Tidewater area of Va., and the eastern half of N. C. The greater part (21) of these are in Type I.

Five informants (three Negro) use the uninflected *take* /tek/, and the following forms occur once each: *tooked* /tukt/ (Pa.), *tooken* /tukən/ (S. C.), *toke* /tok/ (Va.), and *taked* /tekt/ (Ga.).

Among the past participle forms, *taken* is by far the most common. Of the informants who use the preterite *took*, only a scattering use any past participle form other than *taken*.

Informants who use the preterite *taken* nearly always use this form as the past participle as well.

The leveled forms *took-took* occur in all major areas, but are not very common (less than one tenth use them) and show no concentration.

Of the informants who use the preterite *tuck*, about half use the same form as a past participle. Nearly all the others use the combination *tuck-taken*.

Of those who use the preterite *takened*, two thirds level the preterite and the past participle.

The forms *takened-taken* occur in six scattered instances. The following occur from once to five times each: *tuck-take, taken-takened, tuck-takened, toke-takened, took-tooken,* and *take-taken* (Negro).

The expression "was taken sick" is extremely common in a rather broad belt along the coast in the M. A. S. and the S. A. S., gradually becoming less common, and even rare, in the inland areas. The form *taken* is almost universal in this context; there are only six instances of *took* and six of *tuck*. All but three of these variants occur in the southeastern portion of N. C.

Teach (101)

The preterite is recorded in the context "Who (taught) you that?"

The full extent of the variant forms can hardly be determined because of the very large number of informants in all areas who use the verb *learn* in this context (see above).

Those who use *teach* almost invariably give the preterite *taught* /tɔt/. *Teached* /titʃt/ is used, however, by seven N. Eng. informants (four IA, three IIA) and by four Type I informants in Va., N. C., and S. C.

Tear (102)

The past participle is recorded in the context "The road was all (torn) up."

The form *torn* /torn/ or /tɔrn/ is almost universal in cultured speech. Its frequency in the other types may be deduced from the extent of *tore*.

Tore /tor/ or /tɔr/ heavily predominates in n.e. N. Eng. among all the noncultured types. In s. and w. N. Eng. it is somewhat scattered and is much more frequent in the older groups (IA and IIA) than in the younger.

In e. N. Y. and n. N. J. *tore* is rather scattered, but elsewhere in the M. A. S. it is used by a majority of Type I (two thirds in Pa., nine tenths in W. Va.) and by about half of Type II.

In the S. A. S. *tore* (very frequently /to/) is all but universal in Type I and in most areas dominates in Type II as well.

Four cultured informants in e. N. Eng. and two in the M. A. S. use *tore* in this context.

Two W. Va. informants and one Va. informant (Negro) give *tored* /tord/; one Ga. Negro uses the uninflected *tear*.

Throw (32)

The preterite is recorded in the context "He (threw) a (stone, rock) at the dog."

Threw /θru/ occurs among all types in all areas, being particularly prevalent in c. Mass., e. N. Y., and n. N. J. The extent of this form in other areas may be deduced from the frequency of the variants.

Throwed /θrod/ (or often in the S. A. S. /θod/) exists in all parts of the East. It is scattered through N. Eng., except for c. Mass. and part of c. Conn. In n.e. N. Eng. it is used by the majority in Types IA and IB, while about one third of the Type II informants use it. In e. N. Y. and n. N. J. *throwed* is used by only a few Type I informants; elsewhere it predominates more or less strongly in this group, except in the coastal areas of Va. and N. C., where many informants use the verb *chunked* instead. In Type II *throwed* is not dominant; it is not used by more than from one fifth to one third of this group in any area of any size. Two cultured informants, both in n.e. N. Eng., use *throwed*.

The uninflected *throw* /θro/ is used by five informants, including two Negroes. *Thrown* /θron/ occurs once in N. C.

Wake (97)

The preterite is recorded in the context "I (woke) up."

Woke /wok/ is by far the most common preterite form in all major areas, with limitations that will be noted below.

Waked /wekt/ occurs with fair frequency in e. N. Eng. (see Figure 20), the heaviest concentration being in the northeast. It is evidently an older form, for it is given by about one fifth of the A type informants in N. Eng. as opposed to about one eighth of the B type. Seven cultured informants use this form.

In w. N. Eng., N. Y., and the entire Midland (including N. J., Pa., e. O., w. Md., and n. W. Va.), *waked* is extremely rare. In s. W. Va. and the remainder of the South Midland and throughout the South, *waked* is somewhat more common, reaching its greatest frequency in N. C., where it is used by about half of Type I and by a little over one fourth of Type II. There is a tendency in all areas where *waked* occurs toward the substitution of *woke;* this is especially striking in N. C., where *woke* is chosen by the younger informant in about three fourths of the communities of divided usage.[19] However, in N. C. about two thirds of the cultured informants prefer the more old-fashioned form *waked;* everywhere else *woke* predominates in cultivated speech,

though a good many minor variants occur among cultured informants.

Wakened /wekənd/ is used by a scattering of informants in the North and the Midland (though not in the South). It occurs in a few contiguous communities in c. Pa. and the upper Ohio Valley. Five cultured informants use this form.

Awoke /əwok/ is fairly common in s. N. Eng. and adjacent parts of N. Y., rare in the North Midland, and does not occur farther south. Seven cultured informants use this form.

Awakened /əwekənd/ is used by 10 informants (nearly all in N. Y. and N. J.), two of whom are cultured.

In the Pennsylvania German area a very common idiom is "got awake" (see map). Most informants who use this also have other forms, such as *wakened, woke,* and *awoke.*

Other preterite forms that occur in isolation are *woked* /wokt/, *woken* /wokən/, *wake* /wek/, and *awaked* /əwekt/.

Negro informants are not in much better agreement on this verb than cultured informants. *Waked* is most common among them, but *woke, woked,* and *wake* also occur.

Wear (75)

The past participle is recorded in the context "He is (worn) out."

The standard *worn* /worn/ or /wɔrn/ predominates on all levels in s. N. Eng., N. Y., and the northern two thirds of N. J. Elsewhere, except in cultivated speech, it is considerably limited by the variant *wore.*

Wore /wor/ or /wɔr/ is used in n.e. N. Eng. by about three fourths of the Type IA informants and by about half the other noncultured informants. In s. N. Eng., e. N. Y., and n. N. J. *wore* is given by less than one third of the Type I informants; elsewhere in the M. A. S. and the S. A. S. its frequency in this group varies from about two thirds (Pa.) to more than nine tenths (N. C.). *Wore* is given by a negligible number of Type II informants in s. N. Eng. and e. N. Y.; elsewhere by from one fourth (Va.) to two thirds (Md. and W. Va.) of this group. Three cultured informants in N. Eng., three in the M. A. S., and one in the S. A. S. use *wore.*

---

[19] Informants who comment on *waked* almost universally regard it as "old," "old-fashioned," or the like.

Write (100)

The past participle is recorded in the context "I have (written) a letter."

The standard *written* /rɪtən/ strongly predominates in cultured speech, and it exists in the other types, though considerably limited by the variant forms.

Wrote /rot/ is used by something less than one third of the informants in N. Eng. About one half each of Types IA and IB use this form, about one fourth each of Types IIA and IIB—indicating that *wrote* is more of an uneducated form than an older form. However, four informants of Type IIIA use *wrote* as the past participle.

Outside of N. Eng. *wrote* predominates in Type I everywhere, the proportions ranging from about three fifths (N. Y.) to well over nine tenths (N. C.). It also prevails in Type II in most areas. Eight cultured informants in the M. A. S. (five in Pa.) and three in the S. A. S. give *wrote* as the past participle form.

Writ /rɪt/ occurs a few times in the Merrimack Valley and elsewhere in n.e. N. Eng. In c. W. Va. this form occurs in four or five contiguous communities; elsewhere in the M. A. S. and the S. A. S. it occurs only in isolation, and rarely.

Wroten /rotən/, apparently a blend showing hesitation between *wrote* and *written*, occurs once in N. Eng. The uninflected *write* is used by two Negro informants.

II. PERSONAL FORMS OF THE PRESENT INDICATIVE

I says 'said' (14)

In N. Eng., only, the first person singular form is recorded as a narrative form in reporting conversations, in such contexts as "I (said) to him" and "(Said) I."

In n. N. Eng. *says* /sɛz/ (*I says*, or, much more frequently, *says I*) occurs in nearly every community. It is used freely by both old-fashioned and modern informants, though not commonly by cultured ones. In s. N. Eng. (except for Cape Cod and the islands) this form is considerably less common and is more clearly characteristic of old-fashioned speech. Here the order is usually *I says* rather than *says I*.

I work, we work (13)

In N. Eng. the first person forms are recorded in the contexts "I (work) all day" and "We (work) all day."

The inflected form *I works* does not occur in N. Eng., though one informant gives *we works* and one, *they works* /wɜks/.

These items were not regularly used in the M. A. S. and the S. A. S.; however, 53 field records, scattered through all parts of the S. A. S., were made before the items were eliminated from the work sheets. The results, though not conclusive, are highly suggestive.

Of the 36 Type I informants who give a response, four (Va., N. C., S. C.) use the inflected form *I works;* 10 (more than one fourth of this group) use it in the plural, *we works*. Of the five Negroes who respond, two give *works* (for both singular and plural), two give *work,* and one gives both forms interchangeably. None of the 12 Type II and cultured informants use *works*.

We might state tentatively that *we works* is fairly common in Type I in the S. A. S., that *I works* occasionally occurs, and that both are in pretty general use among the more old-fashioned Negroes.

I have (12–13)

The first person singular of *have* as the principal verb is recorded in the context "I (have) my troubles," and of *have* as an auxiliary verb in the contexts "I (have) been thinking" and "I (have) heard it."

In "I (have) my troubles," *have* /hæv/ (or commonly /hɛv/ in N. Eng.) is, with negligible exceptions, the only form recorded, though *got* frequently appears (*I've got* or *I got*). Only two white informants, both in Md., give the form *has* /hæz/, and three Negro informants (Va. and N. C.) use this form.

In "I (have) been thinking" the usual form is *I've* /aiv/, though the /v/ is frequently lost by assimilation. One informant in Pa. and 19 in the S. A. S. (including three Negroes) use the form *I'm* /aim/ ("I'm been thinking"). Nearly all of these informants are in or near the Chesapeake Bay area, and all but two fall in Type I.

In "I (have) heard it before," *I've* is almost universal (with /v/ retained). Nineteen informants in the S. A. S. use *I'm* in this context ("I'm heard," or *heered*, or *heern*—see above, p. 16). With three exceptions these are the same informants as those who use *I'm* in "I've been thinking."

I be, he be, etc. (24, 42–43, 92)

The present tense personal forms of *to be* are recorded in the contexts "(Am) I going to get some?," "(Are) they going to get some?," "He isn't as tall as I (am)," "I'm not as tall as he (is)," and "How (are) you?"

The form *be* /bi/ occurs sporadically and inconsistently in these contexts throughout most of N. Eng. and the N. Eng. settlement area (N. Y. and n. Pa.), as shown on Figure 21. It is completely missing from the Midland and the Southern areas.

Be occurs most frequently in the phrase "How are you?," where it is particularly common in n.e. N. Eng.[20] Of the 56 spontaneous occurrences which I count in N. Eng., 40 are in the northeast. *Be* is very characteristically an older form, both in N. Eng. and in those areas of N. Y. and Pa. where it occurs. Except for *be, are* (frequently pronounced /ær/ by older informants) is the only form current in the East in this context, though there is one occurrence of *is* /ɪz/ ("How is you?") from a N. C. Negro.

In "tall as I am," *be* is a little less frequent than it is in the preceding phrase, but, as the map shows, it extends a little farther south in N. J. and Pa. It is even more characteristically an older feature; of 28 N. Eng. informants who use it, 21 fall in Type IA and four in IIA. Outside of N. Eng. nearly all of the users are in Type I. No other variants of *am* are recorded in the East.

In "tall as he is," *be* occurs only three times in N. Eng. (all in Type IA), twice in n. Pa.,[21] and twice in n. and w. N. Y.

In "Am I going?" *be* occurs in scattered fashion in N. Eng., two thirds of the occurrences being in Type IA. Two Type I informants in n.w. Pa. use *be* in this context. In the South *is* has considerable currency in this phrase among Type I informants.

This form is particularly common in e. Va., where more than half of the Type I informants use it. A scattering of Type I informants in N. C. and S. C. also use *is*, and more than half of the Southern Negro informants do so.

In "Are they going?" *be* shows about the same distribution as it does in the phrase above, but considerably less frequency. *Is* appears in the South in this phrase, also, but much less frequently than it does in the preceding phrase; however, almost as many Negroes use *Is they?* as *Is I?*[22]

In addition to the occurrences already mentioned, some of the fieldworkers record instances of *be* as a present indicative in various conversational contexts. It is not practical to analyze these instances, except to point out that they occur in syntactic and prosodic positions where stress might be expected. These occurrences all fall within the area of *be* indicated in Figure 21, but are not themselves entered on the map.

He does (12)

The third person singular of *do* is recorded in the three contexts "He (does) it all the time," "(Does) he do that sort of thing?," and "He (does)" (emphatic).[23]

In N. Eng. and the M. A. S. the inflected form *does* /dʌz/ is universal with only three exceptions. In N. Eng. this form is often pronounced /dʊz/ by older informants, particularly in the northeast. There are five instances of /dʊz/ in N. Eng. and three in the S. A. S. Otherwise, the vowel of *does* is universally /ʌ/, /dʌz/.

In the Piedmont and Tidewater areas of Va., part of e. N. C., S. C., and Ga. the uninflected form *do* /du/ occurs fairly commonly in all of these contexts (see Figure 22). A large majority of the users fall into Type I. Not all of them use it in all of the items (though most of them do); however, *do* is about equally frequent in all three of the contexts in which it is recorded.[24]

Of the Southern Negro informants, all but one

---

[20] Cf. *Handbook*, pp. 16 and 37. I have noted more occurrences of "How be you?" in Me. than are entered on Chart 22 of the *Handbook* (p. 37).

[21] Some of the material is missing for N. J., N. Y., Pa., and W. Va.

[22] Note that in "I'm going today," where the verb is an auxiliary without stress, neither *be* nor *is* occurs among the Eastern informants.

[23] The first person singular of the same verb was also recorded, in the context "I (do) it all the time." Here *do* is universal: there are no instances of *I does* or any other inflected form.

[24] McDavid recorded *do* for the third person singular in various contexts; these occurrences, also, are presented in Figure 22.

(Md.) use the uninflected *do* in at least one of the contexts, and most use it in more than one.

He doesn't (13)

The third person singular of the negative form is recorded in the context "He (doesn't) care."

In contrast to the positive form (*does*), the negative form lacks the inflectional -*s* /z/ among a large majority of informants in all areas.

In N. Eng. *he don't* /dont/ is used by about two fifths of the cultured informants (mostly in the older group) and by more than five sixths of the other types. It is most common in Type IA (nearly nine tenths use it) and decreases in frequency in proportion to the youth and better education of the informants, occurring among only 6/17 of Type IIIB.

In the M. A. S. *he don't* is all but unanimous in Types I and II, there being but 15 or 20 occurrences of *doesn't* in these groups. Of the cultured informants, nearly three fourths use *he don't* (in a few instances alongside *doesn't*). Cultured informants who use only *doesn't* are mostly to be found in or near New York City or Philadelphia.

In the S. A. S., also, *don't* is universal in Types I and II. About half of the cultured informants use *don't*, occasionally alongside *doesn't*.

What makes (13)

The third person singular form is recorded in the S. A. S. and part of the M. A. S. in the context "What (makes) him do it?"

The uninflected form *make* /mek/ (or sometimes /mɛk/) appears in the S. A. S. in a distribution strikingly similar to that of *he do* (see above). *What make* reaches a little farther west at some points than *he do*, but it is not so frequent in S. C. and Ga. (see Figure 23). *Make* is primarily a Type I form, though about one fourth of the occurrences are in Type II, and two cultured informants in Va. use this form. About two thirds of the Negro informants who give a response use *make* in this context.

He looks like, favors, etc. (65)

The third person singular form is recorded in the context "He (looks like) his father." Although the verb used varies (*favors, resembles, takes after,*

and so on), it was presumably always recorded with the subject *he*.

There are only 11 informants, all in the coastal South (five Negro), who give the uninflected form of the verb. In all of these instances the verb chosen was *favor: he favor* /fevə/; three Negroes use both *he favor* and *he look like*.

She rinses (18)

The third person singular form is recorded in the context "She (rinses) the dishes."

The inflection -*es* /əz/ is almost universal, giving the forms *rinses* /rɪn(t)səz/, *renses* /rɛn(t)səz/, and (as a predominant form in the Midland and the South) *renches* /rɛntʃəz/.

In N. Eng. there are eight scattered occurrences of the uninflected form *rinse* /rɪnts/, and two S. C. Negro informants use this form. *She rench* /rɛntʃ/ is used by three white informants in the S. A. S. and by six Negroes. Of the Negroes who give a response, over one third fail to inflect this verb.

It costs (94)

The third person singular form is recorded in the context "It (costs) too much." Data is not available for N. Eng.

The inflected form with /s/ is universal in the M. A. S. and strongly predominant in the S. A. S. Of course, phonetic reductions of the types [-sts, -ss, -ˢˢ, -s] are extremely common everywhere; the simple [-s] (/kɔs tu mʌtʃ/) is more common in the S. A. S. than in the M. A. S.

A variation from the usual inflectional pattern (/s/ after voiceless consonants) is seen in the form *costes* /kɔstəz/, which occurs occasionally in the Chesapeake Bay area, s. W. Va., N. C., S. C., and Ga. All together, 54 informants (51 of them in Type I) use this form. A similar form, *cosses* /kɔsəz/, is used by nine additional Southern informants.

III. NUMBER AND CONCORD

You were (13)

The second person preterite form is recorded in the context "You (were) talking to him."

In N. Eng. about one fourth of the informants use the plural form *were* /wər/, and an additional one fifth use this form alongside the singular *was*

/wəz/. *Were* is far more common in s. N. Eng. than in the northeast, where *was* is nearly universal. The plural is clearly the newer form, occurring almost invariably among the more modern informants in communities where usage is divided. No cultured informant uses only *was*, though three give this form alongside *were*.

In the M. A. S. *was* is practically universal in Types I and II (more than nine tenths of both groups use it), but is rare in cultured speech (four occurrences are recorded). Two Quaker informants in s.e. Pa. state that *thee was* would be used in addressing a friend.

In the S. A. S., also, *was* is practically universal in Type I (over nine tenths use it), and it is strongly predominant (three fourths use it) in Type II. Only four cultured informants (Va. and N. C.) give the form *was*.

We were (13, 25)

The first person plural of the preterite form is recorded in N. Eng. in the context "We (were) talking to him" and in the M. A. S. and the S. A. S. in the context "We (were) going to do it."

In N. Eng. the distribution of *we was* is very close to that of *you was*. Some 20 more informants use *were* with *we* than with *you*.

In the M. A. S. and the S. A. S. *we was* predominates in Type I (over three fourths use it) and Type II (two thirds use it), as does *you was*. Seven cultured informants in these areas use the singular form *was* with *we*.

People think (13)

The present tense plural form is recorded in the context "People (think) he did it."

In N. Eng. the plural form *think* /θɪŋk/ is almost universal in all types (nine tenths use it) in the southern and western areas, including all of Vt. Northeast of the Merrimack, however, as well as on Nantucket and Martha's Vineyard, the singular *thinks* /θɪŋks/ is used by nearly all the noncultured informants. In s.e. N. H. and n.e. Mass. there is a small transition area where the two forms are about equally common. Only one cultured informant (Me.) uses *thinks*.

In the M. A. S. and the S. A. S. the singular *thinks* is the universal popular form, being used by

nine tenths or more of both Type I and Type II. In the M. A. S. this form has some currency in cultured speech (about one third use it); in the S. A. S., as in N. Eng., it is rare in this type of speech.

They say (13)

In the M. A. S. and the S. A. S. the present tense plural form is recorded in the context "They (say) he did it."

In contrast to the predominant use of the singular in *people thinks*, the plural form *say* /se/ is almost universally used with *they* in the context specified. There are only 14 occurrences of *says* /sɛz/, scattered very widely through the S. A. S.

Although material for comparison is not available, it should be noted that the distribution of *says* in this phrase does not necessarily have any resemblance to that of the narrative form *says* (= 'said'—see above, p. 26).

Here are (25)

The present tense form is recorded in the context "Here (are) your clothes."

In N. Eng. the singular contracted form *here's* /hirz/[25] is used by about four fifths of the noncultured informants. Those who use *are* are mostly to be found in s. N. Eng. and are predominantly of the more modern types. In some eight instances *here are your* cannot be distinguished from *here your* [hiə jə].

In the M. A. S. and the S. A. S. *here's* is universal in Type I and almost so in Type II (nine tenths use it).

In N. Eng. and the S. A. S. about half the cultured informants use the singular *here's;* in the M. A. S. a little over one third do so.

There are (25)

The present tense form is recorded in the context "There (are) many people who think so."

The singular form *there's* (/ðərz/, /ðɛrz/, and so on) is heavily predominant in all areas except in cultured speech. Its distribution is very similar to that of *here's* in the preceding item.

In N. Eng. about 30 more informants use *there are* than use *here are;* in the M. A. S. and the

---

[25] There are, of course, very many variations in the pronunciation of *here* throughout the East.

S. A. S. the former is slightly more common than is *here are* (though still negligible) in Types I and II. A majority (from two thirds to three fourths) of the cultured informants in all areas use the plural form *there are*.

A variation that occurs with some frequency (in about half the communities) in W. Va. and the Chesapeake Bay area is "it's many people," /ɪts/ or /hɪts/ being used instead of *there's*. This is about as common in Type II as in Type I, and three cultured informants use *it's* in this context.

Oats are (42)

The present tense form is recorded in the context "Oats (are) thrashed."

In N. Eng. the plural form *are* /ər/ or /ə/ is all but universal except for part of s. Me. and n. N. H., where *is* /ɪz/ is fairly common. Of the 50-odd occurrences of *is* in N. Eng., four fifths are among the older (IA and IIA) informants.

In the M. A. S. *is* is the dominant form in Type I (three fourths use it) and Type II (three fifths use it). In e. N. Y., n. N. J., and n. Pa. this form is somewhat scattered and is more or less confined to Type I; in the remainder of the M. A. S. it is nearly universal among noncultured informants. Fourteen cultured informants use the singular verb form here.

In the S. A. S. *is* predominates in Type I (about three fourths use it), but is not very common in Type II, being used by less than one fourth of this group; and only four cultured informants use it in this construction.

Except in the Midland it appears that the singular verb is receding rapidly.

Cabbages are (55)

The present tense form is recorded in the context "Those cabbages (are) big."

Is in this context is considerably less frequent than in the preceding item, *oats are*.

When the inflected noun plural *cabbages* is used, all N. Eng. informants say *are*. In the M. A. S. and the S. A. S. between two fifths and one half of the Type I informants, and most of the Southern Negroes, use *is*. This form is least frequent in N. Y. and most frequent in W. Va. Very few Type II informants (less than one seventh in the M. A. S.,

less than one twentieth in the S. A. S.) use the singular verb form in this construction, and no cultured informant uses it.[26]

IV. NEGATIVE FORMS

Am not (25)

The present tense negative form is recorded in the contexts "I (am not) going to hurt him" and "I'm right, (am I not)?"[27]

In the first of these statements *I ain't* /ent/ and *I hain't* /hent/ are given by less than half the N. Eng. informants, most of whom choose *I'm not*. *Ain't* and *hain't* are most common in the old-fashioned groups and tend to be avoided by the more modern. *Ain't* predominates over *hain't* by 10 to one. There is no particular concentration of these forms in N. Eng., but they are least commonly recorded in R. I. and c. Mass.

In New York City, the northern half of N. J., the lower Hudson Valley, and the northern part of e. O., *ain't* is not recorded at all, all informants choosing the *I'm not* construction instead. Everywhere else in the M. A. S. and the S. A. S. *ain't* (or *hain't*) is used by from four fifths (Pa.) to over nine tenths (Va. and N. C.) of Type I and by from one third (W. Va.) to four fifths (Va. and N. C.) of Type II.

Six cultured informants in N. Eng., two in the M. A. S., and three in the S. A. S. use *I ain't*.

Except for a few communities along the upper Susquehanna, *hain't* for *am not* is very rare and isolated in the M. A. S. and the S. A. S. (22 occurrences all together).

Ain't (or *hain't*) *I?* is somewhat more frequent in N. Eng. in the query "I'm right, am I not?" than *I ain't* is in statements, being used by about three fifths of all informants. Ten cultured informants in N. Eng. use *ain't I?*, usually along with some other form.

In the areas mentioned above where *I ain't* is not recorded, *ain't (hain't) I?* is extremely common— practically universal in Type I and strongly predominant in Type II as well. Elsewhere in the M. A. S. and the S. A. S., in Types I and II, *ain't (hain't) I?* is about as universal as a form can be.

---

[26] *Cabbage* is often uninflected in the plural, so the phrase frequently runs "Them cabbage are," and so on.
[27] The interrogative *ain't* was not regularly recorded by McDavid.

Hain't I? is a little more common than *I hain't* (see above), but is still nothing like so common as *ain't I?*, and shows no concentration except to some extent along the Susquehanna and in n.w. N. C.

Nearly one third of the cultured informants in the M. A. S. and the S. A. S. use *ain't I?*, usually alongside some other form.

There are about a dozen occurrences of the form *een't* /int/, nearly all in the coastal areas of Va. and N. C.

The reason why *I ain't* is less frequently recorded than *ain't I?* is very probably that in such a statement as "I am not going to hurt him," the informant is easily able to avoid what he feels to be a disapproved form by means of the perfectly natural *I'm not*, whereas in "I'm right, am I not?" he is syntactically trapped and must use either *ain't* or something worse. Informants in the South seem to be least inhibited about the use of *ain't*, those in R. I. and the New York City area, most inhibited.

Those who avoid *ain't I?* usually choose *am I not?* This construction is particularly common in s. N. Eng., where it occurs in all types (though mostly among younger informants). Elsewhere it is uncommon except in cultured speech. In N. Eng. *am I not* is used by 26/41 cultured informants, in the M. A. S. and the S. A. S. by about the same proportion. A good many of these informants also use *ain't*.

Aren't /ɑrnt/ *I?* is rare in all areas. It is used by 23 N. Eng. informants, only five of whom are cultured. In the entire M. A. S. and S. A. S. *aren't I?* is used by only seven informants, none very far from the coast. Two of these are cultured.

Have not (12, 40)

The present tense negative form is recorded in the contexts "I (haven't) done it" and "I (haven't) done nothing."[28] Lowman's practice in the M. A. S. and the S. A. S. seems to have been to record the phonetic form of *haven't* (if the informant knew such a form) in the first of these contexts, and the variants of *haven't* in the second. By a comparison of the data for the two items, we can determine that nearly all informants in the East know and use the form *haven't* (/hævənt/, with various as-similative changes) alongside the variants to be mentioned.

The negative contraction in "I (haven't) done nothing" is not recorded regularly in N. Eng. except in Me. and N. H.[29] Here the forms *ain't* /ent/ or *hain't* /hent/, or both, are used by nearly all informants, in about equal numbers. A comparison of the forms in the other context, "I (haven't) done it," enables us to determine that these same forms occur in all parts of N. Eng., though they are somewhat uncommon in parts of s. N. Eng. *Hain't* is a little more common than *ain't*, but it is slightly the more old-fashioned of the two.

In the M. A. S. a considerable majority of Type I (seven eighths) and Type II (two thirds) informants use either *ain't* or *hain't* in "I (haven't) done nothing." *Hain't* is slightly more frequent in Type I, *ain't* in Type II. There is no striking geographical distribution, except that *hain't* (rather than *ain't*) is almost universal in n.e. Pa.

In the S. A. S. nearly all informants in Type I (over nine tenths) and most in Type II (three fifths) use either *ain't* or *hain't*, the latter being less common but occurring in heavier proportions in Type I than in Type II. The Piedmont area of Va. is clearly marked by the absence of *hain't;* in all other parts of the S. A. S. the two forms occur side by side.

Three informants give the form *heen't* /hint/, and six (two Negro) use *een't* /int/.

Three cultured informants in N. Eng give the form *hain't* alongside *haven't;* in the M. A. S. and the S. A. S. *ain't* is the only variant of *haven't* recorded in this type (five times in the M. A. S., once in the S. A. S.).

It should be noted that the distribution of *hain't* in "I (haven't) done nothing" is entirely different from that in "I (am not) going to hurt him" (see above, p. 30). More than 330 Eastern informants use *hain't* meaning 'have not'; less than 40 use it meaning 'am not.' We may conclude that, although a large number of informants use *ain't* in both contexts, those who use *hain't* usually use it only to mean 'have not,' distinguishing it from *ain't* 'am not.'

---

[28] This item was also designed to help in establishing the extent of the double negative.

[29] Lowman was the only fieldworker who recorded *have not* regularly in this context. All the others recorded double negatives regardless of context.

Was not (25)

The preterite negative form of *to be* is recorded in the context "It (wasn't) me."

The form *wan't* (pronounced /wɑnt/, /wɔnt/, and sometimes /wont/) shows a striking geographical distribution (see Figure 24). Throughout N. Eng., except for R. I., parts of c. and w. Mass., and s. Vt., this form is extremely common—almost universal northeast of the Merrimack. It appears among all types of informants, including one fourth of the cultured group. In N. Y. and n. Pa. it also appears in a good many communities, usually among Type I informants only. In the Southern area *wan't* is very solid in e. Va., extending inland to the Blue Ridge, and almost as common in e. N. C., though along the coast several informants use *weren't* instead. It is used fully as often by Type II informants as by Type I, and by half the cultured group in this area. It is certainly not an "illiterate"[30] form, but informants who comment on it regard it as "old-fashioned," "familiar," or "careless," though "natural."

The form *weren't* /wɜnt/ is found in several communities in coastal N. C., and there are a few scattered occurrences elsewhere.

Warn't /wɑrnt/ or /wɔrnt/ is not very common anywhere, being found only in scattered communities, mainly along the Southern coast and in w. N. C. and w. Va.

The unusual form *werdn't* /wɜdnt/ or /wɜtnt/ occurs five times in Delmarva and once on the lower Susquehanna.

The assimilation of /z/ to /d/ before /n/—/wɑdənt/, /wʌdənt/,—is recorded a number of times in the South Midland and in S. C.—and it shows up a few times in n. and w. N. Y. It is most common in the records of McDavid, who picked it up mainly in rapid conversation.

Do not (49, 98)

The negative contraction is recorded in the contexts "I (don't) care for any" and "(Don't) you touch it!"

The only contracted form in general use is *don't* /dont/, with, of course, frequent assimilative changes, such as [doŋkɛr] or [dontʃə]. There are five instances of /dʌnt/ in N. Eng.; otherwise the vowel of this form is universally /o/.

As has been shown (p. 28), the form *don't* is general in the third person *(he don't)*, as well as in the other persons.

Will not (58)

The present tense negative form is recorded in the context "I (won't) do it."

A few informants in N. Eng., mostly in w. Conn. and the Boston area, use *shan't* /ʃænt/ or /ʃɑnt/ in this context; elsewhere only some reduced form of *will not* is in use.

In the M. A. S. (except N. Y. and n. Pa.) and the S. A. S. *will not* contracts to /wont/, the variants being uncommon and scattered. The form /wont/ is also fairly common in s. N. Eng., especially among more modern informants.

In N. Eng., N. Y. (except the lower Hudson Valley), and n. Pa. the usual form is /wʌnt/ (see Figure 25). It is almost universal in the area indicated, except that in s. N. Eng. it occurs side by side with /wont/.

The Greater New York City area—including w. Long Island, the lower Hudson Valley, and e. N. J.—sets itself off from the remainder of the North by the use of the form /wunt/. Within this area nearly all informants (including 8 of the 12 cultured) use this form; outside of this area it is very rare in the M. A. S. In the S. A. S. /wunt/ is rather scattered, except in Charleston and a small surrounding area, where it is the predominant usage. Its use by a good many cultured informants would indicate that it is a "prestige form" in this locality.

The form /wʊnt/ is rare except in Martha's Vineyard, Nantucket, and e. Long Island, where it is in general use, and in coastal S. C., where it occurs alongside /wunt/.

The form /wɔnt/ occurs in a few scattered communities in s. Pa., and somewhat more commonly, though without great concentration, in N. C.

Ought not (58)

The negative form of *ought* is recorded in the context "He (oughtn't) to."

In the southern two thirds of Pa. and nearly

---

[30] It is classified as "illiterate" in S. A. Leonard's survey, *Current English Usage.* For a reprint of this material, see A. H. Marckwardt and Fred G. Walcott, *Facts about Current English Usage* (New York: Appleton-Century, 1938), pp. 65–137. The context in which *wan't* was judged in the Leonard survey was "My cold *wan't* any better the next day." Marckwardt and Walcott classify the form as "dialect," without attempting to indicate its level (p. 57).

everywhere to the southward *oughtn't* /ɔtənt/ is in universal use in all types. In the South Midland and throughout N. C. phonetic, and probably phonemic, /r/ very generally appears in this form: /ɔrtənt/.

In N. Eng., N. Y., n. Pa., and most of N. J. the usual form is *hadn't ought* (see Figure 26). Throughout most of this area nearly all the non-cultured informants use this form; however, in s. N. Eng. only about half the informants use it, often alongside *oughtn't* or *ought not*. One third of the cultured informants in N. Eng. (nearly all of those who were interviewed in the northeast) use *hadn't ought*. There are only three instances of *didn't ought* in N. Eng.

In a small area of s. Ohio extending northeast from Marietta, and in part of n.e. N. C. *hadn't ought* is also current, though not universal.

Dare not (58)

The negative form is recorded in the context "You (dare not) go."

Most cultured informants lack a negative contraction of this verb, and about half the noncultured in s. N. Eng. fail to give such a form. Elsewhere the contracted forms are used by most to nearly all Type I and Type II informants.

The form *dasn't* /dæsənt/ is more common than any other contracted form in N. Eng.; and in N. Y. (including New York City and Long Island) it is almost the only such form in use. It occurs in a scattered way in the remainder of the East, being particularly common in s. Ohio, but it is apparently basically a Northern form.

Daresn't /dærsənt/ or /dɛrsənt/ occurs about as often as *dasn't* in w. N. Eng.; in the Midland, except for areas to be indicated, it is clearly the dominant form. *Daresn't* (or a phonetically similar form) also occurs fairly commonly in the Tidewater area of the South and in nearly all parts of N. C., with certain peculiarities that will be noted.

Darsn't /dɑ(r)sənt/[31] is found in a scattered way in most parts of the East, but it also shows concentration in certain well-marked areas. In Me. (except for the s.w. corner), w. Pa., and the Piedmont area of Va. it is heavily predominant over

other contracted forms. It also occurs as often as any other form in e.c. and s. W. Va.

In all the forms mentioned so far /z/ occasionally occurs instead of /s/: /dæznt/, /dærznt/, /dɑ(r)znt/. The voiced consonant is particularly common in e. Va., but occurs now and then in other parts of the S. A. S., as well as a few times in N. Eng.

Daren't /dɛrənt/ or /dærənt/ is uncommon in the East, appearing in the speech of less than 35 informants, seven of whom are cultured. This form shows no concentration except in part of w. Conn.

Durstn't /dɜsənt/ is even more rare, there being but seven widely scattered occurrences.

In N. Eng. and the M. A. S. the usual grammatical construction is "You dasn't (etc.) go." In the S. A. S., however, *to* /tə/ usually precedes *go*, and the resulting complications often lead us to doubt that we are actually dealing with a negative contraction. In nearly 60 instances /r/ (as [ɚ], [ə], or [ə]) clearly follows *you*, indicating the form *you're;* and the forms that follow, /dærsən tə/ or /dɑ(r)sən tə/, probably represent an *-ing*-type adjective meaning 'afraid,' followed by *to*. One informant (Md.) actually uses [ɪŋ], presumably as a "careful" pronunciation: [jɔə dɛəsɪŋ tə goʊ]. Four N. C. informants have apparently converted this adjective form to *daresome* (= 'scared')— /jur dærsəm tə go/, and four others use /jur dærɪn tə go/, probably representing 'You're darin' (= 'scared' rather than 'daren't') to go.'

Daredn't /dærdənt/ appears four times; at least once it represents an adjective following *you're:* [juɚ dæədn tə].

Some four or five Eastern informants substitute *don't* (or *wouldn't*) *das(t)* to go /dont dæs tə go/ in this phrase.

Didn't use to (74)

The negative form of *used to* is recorded in the context "She (didn't use to) be afraid."

Didn't use to /dɪdənt jus tə/ is almost universal in all areas and among all types. The variants to be noted are found only among a small minority of informants.

The negative contraction *usen't* /jusənt/ occurs with regularity only in a very small area of w. c. Md. and in n. Va. in the general vicinity of Harper's Ferry. There are six occurrences of this form,

---

[31] The /r/ is of course vocalized, usually with lengthening of the preceding /ɑ/, in some areas of the East in which this form occurs. See p. 4, note 14.

divided among Shenandoah and Loudoun counties in Va. and among Carroll, Frederick, and Montgomery counties in Md. Outside of this area there are only three occurrences in the East (Springfield, Mass., New York City, and Catawba Co., N. C.).

Some 50 informants in the S. A. S. (mostly in N. C. and S. C.) use the construction *used to didn't be*. This is most common among Type I and Negro informants.

Exceptional phrases occurring from once to five times each are *used not to be, used to not be, used to be not* (Negro), *used to wuzn't* /wʌzən/, *used to wan't* /wɔnt/, and *wan't used to be* (Negro).

Nine N. Eng. informants and a few informants in N. Y. express the negative with *never: never used to be.*

V. INFINITIVE AND PRESENT PARTICIPLE

To tell (80)

The infinitive is recorded in the context "He came over (to tell) me about it."

The construction *for to tell* /fə(r) tə tɛl/ is used by 23 N. Eng. informants, all but two of whom are in the northeast. This is clearly an older form, 13 of the occurrences falling in Type IA, five in IIA.

For to tell occurs in all major portions of the M. A. S., where it is used by some two fifths of the Type I informants and by a little less than one fourth of the Type II. It is least frequent in e. N. Y. and most frequent in W. Va., where it is used by a majority of both Type I and Type II informants.

In the S. A. S. as far south as N. C. *for to tell* is used by a little over half of the Type I informants, and by a little less than one fourth of the Type II. In S. C. and Ga. it is recorded much less frequently.

Two cultured informants (Va. and W. Va.) use *for to tell.*

Two Negro informants in coastal S. C. and one in coastal Ga. use the abbreviated *for tell.*

Singing and laughing (57)

The present participle forms are recorded in the context "She was (singing) and (laughing)." These two verbs are recorded irregularly and incompletely in N. Eng.; in the M. A. S. and the S. A. S. nearly all informants give forms of these verbs, presumably in the required context.

Two types of participial ending are current: the /-ɪŋ/ type, /sɪŋɪŋ, lafɪŋ/, and the /-ɪn, -ən/ type, /sɪŋɪn, læfɪn/. The alternation is probably primarily a phonological matter.[32] In general, /-ɪŋ/ is a cultured form and /-ɪn/ is the corresponding popular form. However, in some areas, particularly s. N. Eng.,[33] e. N. Y., n. N. J., and s.e. Pa., the /-ɪŋ/ form occurs as often as the /-ɪn/ form in Type II, and even a good many times in Type I. In the remainder of the East (n. and w. Pa., W. Va., and all of the S. A. S.), the /-ɪŋ/ is uncommon in Types I and II: less than one tenth of these groups use it in both verbs.

Cultured informants in N. Eng. and the M. A. S. strongly prefer the /-ɪŋ/ type (about four out of five use it); this class of informants is, however, about equally divided between /-ɪŋ/ and /-ɪn/ in the S. A. S., where, no doubt, either form is acceptable in cultivated speech in most communities.

In the same context, an attempt was made in the M. A. S. and the S. A. S. to record participial forms with the *a-* prefix /ə'sɪŋɪn/, /ə'læfɪn/, if these existed in the informant's speech. In N. Eng. some fieldworkers tried to estimate the frequency of such forms in the informant's conversation without recording them in any specified verb or context, whereas others recorded them only in the phrase "singing and laughing." The results are presented on Map 671 of the *Linguistic Atlas of New England.*

The N. Eng. materials are too complex and irregular for compact summary. They show that *a-singing* and *a-laughing* both occur in n.e. N. Eng., but that the second is more than three times as frequent as the first. Presumably the usual utterance would run: "She was singin(g) and a-laughin(g)." Various verbs with *a-* occur throughout N. Eng. Informants whose speech is judged to be free of this feature are seen (Map 671 of the *Atlas*) to be more frequent in c. and w. Mass. than elsewhere;

---

[32] I.e., it probably applies to any final unstressed /iŋ/, regardless of morphological significance. The /-n/ is, for example, extremely common in *nothing*, where the *-ing* does not represent an inflectional element.

[33] Information on these two verbs in s. N. Eng. is very scanty. For a summary of usage in N. Eng. with regard to /-ɪŋ/ and /-ɪn/, see Map 672 of the *Linguistic Atlas of New England.*

however, there is no area of any extent where the a- forms do not occur, at least occasionally.

In the M. A. S. the forms a-singing and a-laughing are recorded with considerable frequency; they are used by about five eighths of the Type I informants as well as by a little over half of the Type II. These forms are fairly common everywhere except in metropolitan New York City and part of c. and w. Pa.; they are particularly common in W. Va., where nearly all informants of Types I and II use them. There is practically no difference in the frequency of a-singing and a-laughing; those who use one form almost invariably use the other.

In the S. A. S. the form a-laughing is given by some seven eighths of the Type I informants and over half of the Type II. However, a-singing in this phrase is only about one third as frequent, and occurs with regularity only in the Chesapeake Bay area and in w. N. C. In Va. and e. N. C. the statement is usually recorded as "She was singin' and a-laughin'" /sɪŋɪnən ə'læfɪn/.

Very few of the cultured informants (five in the M. A. S., one in the S. A. S.) use the forms with the prefix.

Going (24)

The present participle of go is recorded in the contexts "I am (going) today," "We are (going) today," "Am I (going) to get some?," and "Are they (going) to get some?"

Goin' /goɪn/ is of course much more common than going /goɪŋ/; moreover, in going to there are almost innumerable phonetic reductions of the types [gɔɪntə, gɔɪnə, gonə, gʌnə, gənə], and no attempt will be made to analyze them.

There are 16 occurrences of gwine /gwain/ in N. Eng., all northeast of the Merrimack. Elsewhere in the East this form does not occur until we reach the Chesapeake Bay area (see Figure 27). In Delmarva, e. Va., N. C., S. C., and coastal Ga. gwine becomes fairly common in Type I (one third to one half of the informants in most of the area use it) and also occurs occasionally in Type II. It does not extend beyond the Blue Ridge in Va., but in N. C. it reaches to the westernmost end of the state, and it is scattered throughout S. C. and e. Ga.

A similar form without /w/, /gain/, is current on the Eastern Shore of Va. and in n.e. N. C. around Albemarle Sound and the lower Neuse River.

These forms are about equally common in all the contexts: those who use /gwain/ or /gain/ in "I am (going) today" almost always use it in "Am I (going) to get some?"—and vice versa. However, a few informants in N. C. use I'm going, but we're gwine.

VI. PHRASES

Might could (58)

The phrase might could, in the context "I (might could) do it" (future), is recorded wherever it occurred in the M. A. S. and the S. A. S.

The isogloss of this form is peculiar in that it not only indicates a typical South and South Midland form,[34] but shows the form to be current in the German area of Pa. as well (see Figure 28).

Within the shaded area of Figure 28, Type I informants offer this form with hardly any exceptions, and it is also used by from two thirds (Va.) to practically all (N. C.) of Type II informants as well. Cultured informants as a rule avoid the construction: there are very few instances of it in this type.

A good many informants in the S. A. S. use the form mought rather than might in this phrase. For the distribution of mought, see above, page 18.

Belongs to be (58)

The construction "He belongs to be careful" is recorded wherever it occurred in the M. A. S. and the S. A. S.

Figure 29 shows its geographical distribution. The phrase is seen to occur in a rather scattered way in e. Va. and on the Western Shore of Md.; in southern Delmarva, e. N. C., S. C., and Ga. it occurs with some regularity, almost as commonly in Type II as in Type I.

The meanings recorded for the phrase are 'ought to be careful,' 'needs to be careful,' and 'generally is careful.' Often more than one meaning is current in a single community, and even in the speech of a single informant.

Three white informants and three Negroes use he longs /lɔŋz/. The uninflected form, he belong /bəlɔŋ/, occurs four times, and he long /lɔŋ/, once (Negro).

---

[34] Cf., for example, the distribution of holp and the other forms recorded on Figure 31.

Like to fell (70)

The phrase *like to fell* in the context and meaning "I (almost) fell down" is recorded wherever it occurred in the M. A. S. and the S. A. S.

In the S. A. S. and W. Va. this construction is very nearly universal in Types I and II; exceptions are so rare as to be negligible. The same is true of n. Pa. and of most of N. Y. and N. J. Only in Greater New York City and the southern three fourths of Pa. is this form lacking, or rarely recorded, in the noncultured types.

In the M. A. S. seven cultured informants use *I like to fell,* and one, *I like to have fallen.* In the S. A. S. 13 use *I like to fell,* and eight, *I like to have fallen.*

CONCLUSION

EVALUATION OF DATA

BEFORE attempting to evaluate the Linguistic Atlas materials with regard to contemporary verb usage, we must be aware of certain limitations in the scope and methods of the undertaking itself.

The Atlas survey proposed to investigate and represent the usage of only the most settled and permanent elements in the Eastern population.[1] Thus it cannot be expected to represent the speech of the large foreign-born or foreign-influenced groups in the East,[2] or of the communities which have been recently populated from other parts of the United States, or of that rather large group of Americans who make a practice of migrating from one locality to another. And hence one should not attempt to verify the isoglosses and distributions based on the Atlas materials by observing the usage of other types of informants in the East.

Certain allowances must be made for the methodology. In N. Eng. nine fieldworkers were employed, and it is inevitable that their results should reflect differences in temperament, interest, and interviewing practices. Lowman, who investigated in n.e. N. Eng., showed a keen interest in archaisms and often suggested such forms to the informant if they were not offered spontaneously. Bloch, on the other hand, in his earlier field work in c. and w. Mass., recorded very few archaic verb forms, and even relatively few popular nonstandard forms, with the result that some maps show blank spaces in his territory.[3] Miss Harris chose a relatively large number of educated informants in R. I.,[4] so that nonstandard verb forms are usually rather thinly scattered. Considering these factors, we may perhaps question the sharpness of some of the lines that set off n.e. N. Eng. from the rest of the area; however, there can be little doubt that, on the whole, archaic verb forms are far more frequent there than elsewhere in N. Eng.

There are some differences between the practices of Lowman and those of McDavid which produce rather different results even in the same areas. McDavid's method of recording most morphological items as they naturally turned up in conversation (rather than by questioning) gives us a good many forms that are used in contexts other than those specified in the work sheets. Sometimes these had to be eliminated from consideration in estimating frequencies, since the incidence of a form in one context (e.g., "boughten bread" or "riz bread") would not necessarily coincide with that in similar contexts.

Even in the parts of the M. A. S. and the S. A. S. where a single fieldworker made all of the observations, a certain amount of caution is necessary in interpreting the results. For example, the relative absence of some of the old-fashioned verb forms from a considerable area around New York City is certainly sound evidence of the elimination of rustic features through rigorous classroom training and the spread of citified speech into the surrounding areas—one would hardly expect to hear "I've heern tell" on the streets of New York City. However, the absence of other forms, such as *I ain't* for *I'm not* (see p. 30), may mean that the metropolitan informant is as a rule very much inclined to be on his guard when questioned as to his speech and to avoid elements that are felt to be disreputable, though they may be more or less natural. Occasionally (as with *ain't*) we have some concrete evidence of such a situation: a great many informants in the New York City area use *ain't I?*—a construction in which the substitutes for *ain't* (*am I not* and *aren't I*) are felt to be unnatural and somewhat "high-hat."

---

[1] Every informant had to be a native-born member of the community he represented; in most cases his parents and grandparents were born in the same community as he was, or at least in the same area.

[2] Older elements of foreign derivation, such as the Germans in Pennsylvania and the Dutch in the Hudson Valley, are fully represented in the Atlas survey.

[3] E.g., for *clim* (Figure 5), *see* (Figure 17), and *wan't* (Figure 24).

[4] One fourth (6/24) of the R. I. informants are classed as "cultured," as against about one tenth for N. Eng. as a whole.

It is hardly necessary to observe that the presence or absence of a form in the record of an individual informant is of little significance. When, however, a number of occurrences fall within a given area, we have convincing evidence of the currency of the form in question, at least in one or another of the social groups represented. As a corollary to this idea, we should be aware of the fact that when a form shows up in about half the communities of an area, it is probably not in actuality confined to those communities in which it is recorded. It might well have a limited currency in all, or nearly all, such communities, though the particular informants chosen by the Atlas survey did not happen to use it. In brief, the Atlas materials are a far surer guide to the usage of an area than to that of an individual community.

GEOGRAPHICAL DISTRIBUTION OF THE FORMS

As the survey has made clear, the geographical lines formed by many (if not most) of the verb forms are not at all clear and sharp. Often we are dealing with recessive forms that tend to thin out or disappear in certain areas and to be preserved more fully in others. Sometimes the retreat has gone rather far; sometimes it has only begun. In general, the older forms tend to become uncommon or disappear first in the New York City area (including n. N. J. and the lower Hudson Valley), in parts of e. Pa., and in the more urbanized areas of s. N. Eng. They are preserved longest in n.e. N. Eng. and in the coastal and mountain areas of the South and the South Midland (from s. W. Va. to the southward). A glance at the discussions of *blowed* (p. 6), *catched* (p. 8), *div* (p. 9), *driv* (p. 11), *rid* (p. 19), *sot* (p. 21), *throwed* (p. 25), *wore out* (p. 25), *I ain't* (p. 30), and *for to tell* (p. 34) will be sufficient to indicate the directions of this receding movement for particular forms, as well as some of the stages which it has reached.

There is, however, a group of verb forms which more or less clearly show regional distribution—that is, distribution corresponding to the major settlement and culture areas of the East.

We have rather definite evidence of a Northern area,[5] consisting of N. Eng., N. Y., and approximately the northern one fourth of Pa. and clearly reflecting the path of the new England migrations westward to the Western Reserve on Lake Erie.[6] The lines formed by *clim* (Figure 5) and *see* (Figure 17) are fairly representative. Even clearer is the line of /wʌnt/ for *won't* (Figure 25). *Be* for *am, is,* or *are* (Figure 21) shows approximately the same distribution, as do *et* (Figure 9) and *wan't* for *wasn't* (Figure 24). In none of these instances, it will be observed, does the Northern form occur with regularity in the lower Hudson Valley; this area had a different settlement history[7] and so would not always share the dialect features of the New England westward movement. As far as *won't* is concerned, the Hudson Valley is clearly set off from the Northern area by the predominance of the form /wunt/ (Figure 25). Some of the Northern lines, however, show a more southerly trend toward the coast. *Be* (Figure 21) shows a little currency in n. N. J. (whose population was partly of N. Eng. origin[8]); and the line for *hadn't ought* (Figure 26) bends southward in such a way as to take in not only the New York City area but most of N. J. as well. A somewhat similar line is exhibited by *dove* (Figure 6), with the exception that this form has undoubtedly been advancing on all portions of the front.

Within N. Eng. itself the evidence of regional distribution is not too clear. Not many forms show anything like a well-marked division between Eastern and Western N. Eng.;[9] *waked* (Figure 20) is about the only good example of such a distribution. Northeastern N. Eng., however, is frequently set off from the remainder of the area, either by the much greater frequency of certain forms there (see above) or by forms that are current almost exclusively in that part of the North, such as *gwine* (Figure 27), *riz* (Figure 16), and *driv* (Figure 8). Probably the clearest line separating the northeast

---

[5] Hans Kurath, *A Word Geography of the Eastern United States* (Ann Arbor, Mich.: Univ. Michigan Press, 1949), presents a great many vocabulary items that set off this area.

[6] The most up-to-date and dependable account of westward population movements may be found in Ray A. Billington, *Westward Expansion* (New York: Macmillan, 1949); see especially pp. 290–309. See also T. J. Wertenbaker, *The Founding of American Civilization: The Middle Colonies* (New York: Scribner's, 1938), pp. 119 ff.; Lois K. Mathews, *The Expansion of New England* (Boston and New York: Houghton-Mifflin, 1909), pp. 139 ff.

[7] See Billington, *op. cit.,* pp. 85–89; Wertenbaker, *op. cit.,* pp. 29 ff.

[8] See Wertenbaker, *op. cit.,* pp. 119–61.

[9] See *Handbook of the Linguistic Geography of New England,* ed. Hans Kurath and others (Providence, R. I.: Brown Univ., 1939), pp. 8 ff. and Charts 7–9.

from the remainder of N. Eng. is that formed by
the northeastern *people thinks* (see p. 29) as against
the southern and western *people think*. Since these
lines may be partly accounted for by a difference
in the practices of fieldworkers, and since most of
the forms involved are archaisms, it would not be
wise to lay too much stress on them. Still, collec-
tively, they serve to mark off the northeast as an
area having a considerable body of forms not commonly found elsewhere in the North, and thus they
are of some value as dialect criteria.

The area lying between the Northern and the
Southern speech areas has been termed "Midland"
by Professor Kurath, who gives adequate evidence
of the region's linguistic unity.[10] It corresponds approximately to the Pennsylvania settlements, and
thus comprises the southern three fourths of Pa.,
w. Md., and W. Va. and the western portions of Va.
and N. C.[11] Its extent on the Atlantic coast is
somewhat uncertain, particularly in the area around
New York City. Its limits in the southern portion
are likewise difficult to fix, since the Pennsylvania-
derived populations of w. Va., w. N. C., and s.
W. Va. were subjected to Southern cultural and
linguistic influence.

As compared with the North and the South, the
area is more clearly marked by the absence of popular verb forms than by characteristic usages of its
own. Some of the lines between the North and the
Midland have already been pointed out, and some
of those separating the South from the Midland will
be indicated below. Forms that appear to be primarily Midland are the preterites *clum* (Figure 5)
and *seen* (Figure 17) and the past participle *boilt*
(p. 6). The first two, it will be observed, show
some currency in the Piedmont areas of the South,
particularly in N. C. A form that marks the South
Midland is *dogbit* (Figure 3), which is particularly
common in W. Va. and w. Va., and which extends

to the coast in the area of the Cape Fear and Peedee
rivers. Within the Midland region we find two
forms marking the German area of Pa.: *got awake*[12]
(Figure 20) and *might could* (Figure 28)—the second being found also in the South and part of the
South Midland.

The Southern area includes s. Md. and probably
the remainder of the Chesapeake Bay area, that
portion of Va. lying to the east of the Blue Ridge,
at least the eastern half or two thirds of N. C., and
a preponderant portion of S. C. This area is essentially that of the early plantation culture, which
advanced inland as far as the mountains.[13]

A number of verb lines set off this territory, of
which that for *heern tell* (see Figure 12) is representative. This line passes through c. Del. and
sets off s. Md. from the northern and western portions. Then it swings southward more or less along
the Blue Ridge; to the south of Roanoke it bulges
westward to the headwaters of the New River, then
swings back eastward into c. N. C. A number of
lines of similar trend are compiled on Figure 30,
representing *heern (tell)*, *it wan't me*, and *what
make?*[14] In all these usages we can observe the
same tendency to westward penetration in the area
south of the upper Roanoke River. The distribution of *is I going?* (Figure 21), *he do* (Figure 22),
and *belongs to be* (Figure 29) is seen to be essentially similar. The line formed by *gwine* (Figure
27) is very much the same so far as Va. is concerned, but bends westward in N. C. so as to include
even the western extremities of the state.

Another type of Southern isogloss represents the
advance of Southern forms into the mountains, particularly in s.w. Va. and w. N. C. A number of
lines of this sort are compiled on Figure 31, representing *holp*, *mought*, and *might could*. These
lines, it will be observed, resemble those of the first
group so far as Md. and n. Va. are concerned.
Some of the forms occur west of the Blue Ridge,
but not commonly or consistently, and, uniquely,
the line of *might could* makes an excursion into
Pennsylvania German territory (see above). From

---

[10] See *Word Geography*. Professor Kurath also dis-
cussed this matter in "The Vocabulary of the American
Midland," a paper read at the 1946 summer meeting of the
Linguistic Society of America. Many lexical items are
shown to be characteristically Midland; two of the most
striking are *sook!* (call to cows) and *I want off.*

[11] See Billington, *op. cit.*, pp. 92 ff., 154 ff.; T. J.
Wertenbaker, *The Old South (The Founding of American
Civilization)* (New York: Scribner's, 1942), pp. 164 ff.;
Rupert B. Vance, *Human Geography of the South* (Chapel
Hill: Univ. North Carolina Press, 1935), pp. 40 ff.; John
C. Campbell, *The Southern Highlander and His Homeland*
(New York: Russell Sage Foundation, 1921), pp. 22–49.

[12] Professor Kurath suggests that this is no doubt based
on the Pennsylvania German construction *ich bin wach
warre* (= *geworden*).

[13] See Wertenbaker, *The Old South*, especially pp. 118 ff.

[14] In Figures 30 and 31 the isoglosses have been somewhat straightened, principally by short-cutting in a few
areas where the forms are thinly scattered.

TABLE I*

EASTERN VERB FORMS WITH A DISTINCTIVELY REGIONAL DISTRIBUTION

/ = fairly common to common
. = scattered

	North						Midland				South			
	n.e. N. Eng.	s.e. N. Eng.	w. N. Eng.	N. Y.	n. Pa.	H. V.	Pa.	W. Va.	w. Va.	w. N. C.	C. B.	e. Va.	e. N. C.	S. C.
CHIEFLY NORTHERN														
wun't /want/	/	/	/	/	/									
be for am, etc.	/	/	/	/										
hadn't ought	/	/	/	/	/									
see (pret.)	/	/	/	/	/	.						.	/	.
dove	/	/	/	/	/	/	.							/
et	/	/	/	/	/	/	.	/			/	.	.	/
CHIEFLY MIDLAND														
boilt							.	/	/	/	.	.		/
clum							.	/	/	/	/	.	.	/
seen (pret.)	.	.	.	.	.		.	/	/	/	/	.	.	/
dogbit								/	/	/	.	.		/
CHIEFLY SOUTHERN														
he do								.	/	/	/			
what make†								/	/	/	/			
belongs to be†								/	/	/	/			
freezed								/	/	/	.			
Is I?							.	/	/	/	.			
heern							.		/	/	/	.		
gwine	/							.	.	/	/	/	/	
div	.							.	.	/	/	/	/	
holp†							.	/	/	/	.	.	.	
seed							/	/	/	.	/	/	/	
mought††							/	/	/	.	.	.	/	
riz	/						.	.	/	/	/	/	/	
taken (pret.)							/	/	.	/	/	/	/	
tuck							/	/	/	.	/	/	/	
might could†						/	.	.	/	/	/	/		
NORTHERN AND SOUTHERN														
wan't	/	/	/	.	/						/	/	/	
clim	/	/	/	/	/	.		.	.	.	/	/	.	/
waked	/	.	/	.				/	/	/	/	/	.	
MIDLAND AND SOUTHERN														
heered							/	/	/	/	/	.	/	
eat (pret.)							/	/	/	/	/	.	/	
sweated	.	.	.		.		/	/	/	/	/	/	/	/

* The diagonal in the tabulation means that the form is fairly common to common, i.e., relatively more common, in the areas indicated; of course the frequency of some of the forms (e.g., *holp* and *hadn't ought*) is much greater than that of others (e.g., *be* and *div*). The dot means that the occurrence of the form is scattered; this symbol is also used to designate the currency of a form in only part of the territory indicated, as with *holp*, which in W. Va. is current only in the southern part. "H. V." stands for the Hudson Valley, approximately as far north as Albany, and "C. B." stands for the Chesapeake Bay area, including Delmarva.

† Not recorded in N. Eng.

the upper James and Roanoke rivers, these forms show a spreading into s.w. Va. and w. N. C., and most of them extend into the southernmost portions of W. Va. as well.

Still another type of Southern line, of which there are not many examples, is represented by that of *I taken* (Figure 30), which runs more or less due westward from s. Del., taking in all of Va. and all but the northernmost portion of W. Va. A somewhat similar distribution is seen in the use of *tuck* (Figure 19) and *fit* 'fought' (Figure 10).

Within the Southern territory the Tidewater area is well marked by the preponderance of *clim* (Figure 5), the Norfolk and e. N. C. area by *fout* (Figure 10), the Albemarle Sound area by *hadn't ought* (Figure 26) and by /gain/ 'going' (Figure 27), and the Piedmont area of Va., the most important of the Southern culture centers, by *see* (Figure 17) and *clome* (Figure 5). The last of these forms shows a westward penetration at some points, particularly in the area of the upper Roanoke and New rivers.

I have presented on Table I a summary of the verb forms in the East exhibiting a distinctively regional distribution. The Hudson Valley, which is tentatively grouped with the North, will be seen occasionally to lack the typical Northern forms. The Southern forms, which make up the largest body of items, are arranged so as to show first those that are confined to the focal area, then those that spread westward into the highlands. It can readily be observed that this spreading is most commonly into w. N. C., less commonly into w. Va.; and least commonly into W. Va. The question of whether some of these Southern-influenced areas should be classed as Southern rather than Midland will be deferred until a more complete analysis of the Atlas materials has been carried out.

SOCIAL DISTRIBUTION OF THE FORMS

As has been stated, the types into which the informants have been divided do not represent sharp cleavages between social groups, since American society itself does not have such divisions. Between Types I and III we might expect to find a considerable gap, but Type II is sure to overlap both of the other groups to a considerable extent. It is hardly possible to find an item of linguistic usage that is exclusively rustic (Type I), or exclusively cultured (Type III), or, least of all, exclusively modern popular (Type II). "Standard" usages that prevail among the cultured are always current, at least to some degree, in the other types; rustic forms are often recorded in the speech of younger and better educated informants; and just about all forms that have wide currency in popular speech are to be found, at least occasionally, in the speech of the cultured. With this understanding, we may proceed to some groupings according to the usage of the different social types.

Forms that may be classed as primarily rustic include the following preterites:

axed	drownded	seed
catched	freezed	sot
cotch	frez	swimmed
div	friz	teached
drawed	frozed	throwed
drinked	mought	tuck
driv	riz	

In the same group belong the past participle forms *heern, rid,* and *boilt,* and the forms *I (you, he) be, we works, I'm been thinking, is I?, he do, what make, it costes,* and *gwine.* Some items in these two groups (particularly *frez, cotch, he do,* and *gwine*) are considerably more frequent among Negroes than among white informants. A larger sampling of Negro usage might enable us to classify these and other forms as "characteristically Negro," but the difference would again be one of frequency. I cannot point to any form that is widely current among Negroes that is not also in use among the more rustic of the white informants.[15]

Another group of forms has very wide currency in Type I and somewhat less, though still considerable, currency in Type II. We might classify these forms as "popular," or "popular regional," meaning extensive in the noncultured types but relatively uncommon among the cultured. Many of these, it has been pointed out in the preceding section, are characteristically regional. They include the preterite forms:

---

[15] The speech of the Gullah Negroes, which was hardly touched in the Atlas survey, has been shown to contain a good many unique morphological features, some of which are the result of African influence. See Lorenzo D. Turner, *Africanisms in the Gullah Dialect* (Chicago: Univ. Chicago Press, 1948).

clim	fit 'fought'	rung
clum	fout	see
done	holp	seen
drug	kneeled	set 'sat'
eat	knowed	taken
et	run	

In this group also belong a good many past participle forms that are leveled to the preterite, such as *bit, rode, wore, swelled, broke,* and *tore,* as well as such other features as *you (we) was, people thinks, there's many people, oats is thrashed, ain't, hain't, wan't, hadn't ought, dasn't, daresn't, singin', might could,* and *like to fell.* Some of these such as *ain't I?, wan't, singin',* and *hadn't ought,* show a surprising degree of currency in the cultured group, and even predominate in that type in certain areas. Although, as has been shown, no form is exclusively popular or exclusively cultured, probably the nearest to a shibboleth is *you was,* the almost universal popular form, against *you were,* the almost universal cultured form (see p. 29).

Another group of popular forms is used by something like half of the cultured, and is favored by that type in areas of considerable extent: *laid* 'lay,' *he don't care, knit* (preterite), *here's your clothes,* and *drank* (past participle).

Of still another group of variants we might say that all three types are more or less in agreement in their use; that is, a majority of the cultured informants favor the popular usage. Among these forms are the preterites *pled, fit, sweat, shrunk, dove,* and *dreamt,* and such other expressions as *he was hung* and *didn't use to.* Some of these vary regionally, and cultured usage varies with them. Where *dove, fit,* and *sweat* prevail in popular speech, they prevail in cultured speech; in areas of *dived, fitted,* and *sweated,* the cultured likewise follow the popular preference.

ORIGIN OF THE FORMS

The present survey does not propose to trace the history of the verb forms recorded in the Eastern States. Only a few observations need be made until a fuller study can be undertaken.

One is impressed by the small number of innovations and of forms that are demonstrably American in origin. By far the greater number of forms that are widely used in America are of Early Modern

English origin, and are more or less fully attested (see the *Oxford English Dictionary*) in the written language of the fifteenth to the eighteenth centuries, as well as in the modern British dialects.[16] In this group fall such preterite forms as *riz, blowed, freezed, driv, heered, shrunk, shrinked, throwed, et, eat, drunk, holp, sot, mought, growed, swole, swum, drownded, clum, clome, catched, teached, knowed, begun, run, come,* and *see.* Past participle forms in use in that period include *bit, rid, rode, driv, drove, writ, wrote, het,* and other of the American forms. In this category also belong such usages as *he do, be* (for *am, is,* or *are*), *a-singing* (and the like), *for to tell, you was,* and other expressions where the modern notion of concord is not observed.

A good many other forms that are not recorded, or not unambiguously documented, in Early Modern English have been observed in nineteenth- and twentieth-century British dialects, and may very well have been current in the British speech of our colonial period. Among these forms are the preterites *friz, frez, drinked, done, seen, fout, fit* 'fought,' and the past participles *droven, heern,* and *brung.* Even such unusual formations as *I'm heerd it* and *it werdn't me* have their counterparts in some of the modern British dialects.[17] No attempt will be made here to trace particular forms to specific dialects of seventeenth-century England, since with our present evidence such an attempt would be arduous and probably unsuccessful.[18]

With regard to the types of verb formation current in America, it will be observed that in a great many instances we have evidence of the Early Modern English practice of making "weak" verbs out

of "strong" (or otherwise irregular) verbs: *blowed, heered, shrinked, drinked, throwed, growed, catched, knowed, seed, drawed*—to mention only a few of the more common. For most of the strong verbs examined in this survey, from a handful to a considerable number of informants give the weak forms (e.g., *rised, freezed, swimmed, teached*).

Most of the unconventional strong forms can be explained on one or more of the following grounds: (1) the direct survival of certain Old and Middle English forms which have been eliminated in the standard language, (2) the early establishing of certain patterns of vowel alternation based on these forms, and (3) the analogical extension of these patterns to verbs of other types. Such preterite forms as *clome, et,* and *het* are the regular descendants of forms found in Old or Middle English, or in both, which have been replaced by newer forms in the standard English of America (/ɛt/ is still standard in England).

In verbs of the *rise* class the Old English preterite plural had the same vowel (*i*) as the past participle; because of a strong leveling tendency this vowel was inevitably often extended to the preterite singular in Early Modern English, and hence came into the modern dialects. *Rise : riz, drive : driv, ride : rid,* and *write : writ* are examples of this treatment.[19] The pattern of vowel alternation /ai : ɪ/ (cf. the standard *hide : hid, bite : bit*) then is extended by analogy to other verbs: *dive : div, fight : fit,* and *climb : clim* (see also below).

Another group of verbs in which the vowel of the preterite plural and the past participle was extended to the preterite singular is that containing /ʌ/ before nasal consonants: *rung, drunk, shrunk, swum,* and *clum.* The pattern /ɪ : ʌ/ then produces the analogical forms *bring : brung.*

The alternation /i : ɛ/ was no doubt established early, and by regular phonetic development, in *eat : et, heat : het,* and other verbs (cf. the standard *bleed : bled* and *lead : led*). By analogy, the pattern is extended to *plead : pled* (O.F. *plaid-ier*), *freeze : frez,* and probably other popular usages.[20]

[16] See Joseph Wright, *The English Dialect Dictionary* (6 vols.; London: H. Frowde, 1898–1905). I have also referred to a survey of southern England on Linguistic Atlas principles carried out by Guy S. Lowman in 1934. This material (unpublished) is in the Linguistic Atlas office at the University of Michigan.

[17] Lowman records *I'm heard it* as the regular form in England in a small area of the East Midland centering around Huntingdon, and *werdn't* or *erdn't* /ɜdənt/ in several of the southwestern counties.

[18] Our knowledge of the present-day distribution of dialect features in England is far from complete, and our knowledge of Early Modern English dialects is extremely limited. To argue from present-day distribution that a certain form must have been brought to an American colony from a certain area of England is risky and neglects the possibility that many forms may have become obsolete in certain areas in the course of two or three hundred years. Such a study should be undertaken only after many cautions and much historical research, and preferably only after a complete survey of England on Linguistic Atlas lines.

[19] See Henry Alexander, "The Verbs of the Vulgate in Their Historical Relations," *American Speech,* IV(1929), 307–15.

[20] Although the preterites of the verbs *grease* and *weed* were not called for in the work sheets, Lowman several times records /grɛz/, and once /wɛd/.

As has been indicated, very few forms can be shown to be of American origin. The preterite forms *clim*, *drug*, and *dove* are far more common in America than in England, and may be native to this continent. As concerns the first two, the present tense forms /klɪm/ 'climb' and /drʌg/ 'drag' are pretty well attested in England[21] (with the preterites /klɪmd/ and /drʌgd/). Assuming that these present forms were introduced into the colonies alongside the forms /klaim/ and /dræg/, we might have a situation where meaningless vowel variation in the present was given morphological significance in differentiating the present from the preterite. No doubt, analogy with *rise : riz* (and the like) would sufficiently explain the form *clim;* if this was in use as a present form, its relegation to preterite function would be facilitated by the existence of the /ai : ɪ/ pattern, into which it could be fitted. As for *dove*, analogy with such verbs as *drive* and *ride* is quite sufficient to explain the wide currency of the form.

SOME CHARACTERISTICS OF POPULAR USAGE

Generalizations regarding popular usage of verbs must be made with extreme caution, since every verb offers its own peculiar problems, and every form shows its own unique distribution.

The most striking characteristic of popular treatment of verbs is the leveling of the preterite and the past participle forms. Where both forms are recorded, we always find a large number of informants, predominantly of the old-fashioned type, who make no distinction between the two. The following forms are freely used as both preterites and past participles: *drove, shrunk, growed, et, eat, drank, drunk, drinked, taken, tuck,* and *swelled.* In some usages where only the preterite is recorded, the forms *swum, rung, seen,* and *done* probably represent leveling, as do the past participle forms *rode, rid, wore, wrote,* and *broke.* Some of these leveled forms (e.g., *shrunk* and *drank*) are common, if not predominant, among all three types of informants in most areas. In nearly all parts of the East the leveled forms of most verbs are predominant in Type I speech, whereas Type II speech is highly variable in this respect, tending to level the forms of some words (e.g., *drink*) far more generally than those of others (e.g., *take*).

It will be observed that in most levelings the standard preterite form serves as both preterite and past participle in popular speech. However, sometimes the standard past participle does so; this is particularly true of verbs of the series /ɪ : æ-ʌ/ before nasal consonants: *rung, begun, swum,* and so on. A notable exception is found in the verb *drink,* where the almost universal leveled form, particularly in the Northern area, is *drank.* Probably *drunk* as a verb form was eliminated because of semantic conflict with the adjective form *drunk* 'intoxicated.' In a few other usages, such as *seen, done, taken,* and (for a small number of informants) *swollen,* the standard past participle form also serves as the popular preterite form. In general, however, this phenomenon is rare.[22]

As has been indicated (p. 42), the leveling of preterite and past participle is of early origin, and was probably widely current in the colloquial English of the Early Modern period. In more recent times there has undoubtedly been a trend toward distinguishing the forms, due to education or the influence of the more highly educated. This "unleveling" process probably accounts for some interesting facts of current usage. As has been shown (pp. 23–24), the preterite forms *tuck* and *taken* occupy approximately the same area, within which *taken* is demonstrably the newer form. It seems highly probable that speakers in this area, through imperfect teaching or otherwise, began to avoid *I have tuck* and to substitute *I have taken* as an elegancy of speech, without understanding its grammatical significance. Thus its use in the preterite would be inevitable, since its users had no true distinction between preterite and past participle. A similar process may ultimately account for *seen* as a preterite form. In *swollen, swoled,* and *swole,* where either the past participle or the vowel of the past participle has in recent times been invading the preterite (see p. 22), we must also be dealing with a hypercorrection, based on the feeling that the past participle form *swollen* is somehow more elegant than the leveled preterite and past participle form *swelled.*

---

[21] *Drug : drugged* is "common from *c* 1500 in Sc.; also in mod. Eng. dialects"—*Oxford English Dictionary. Clim : climmed* is recorded by Wright, *op. cit.,* in a large number of English counties.

[22] E.g., there are no instances of *driven, given,* or *drawn* as preterites, and only one each of *known, thrown,* and *frozen.*

There is no evidence that the standard preterite and past participle forms are habitually reversed in popular speech.[23] Although there are scattered instances of the combinations *drunk-drank* and *shrunk-shrank* (pp. 11, 21), they are too few to be of any significance, and other combinations of this sort are almost, or entirely, nonexistent. The true situation seems to be that many informants waver between two forms, either of which may serve as preterite or as past participle. Thus reversal of the standard forms might occur on occasion, but not as a regular feature unless in the speech of rare and atypical individuals.

In a number of verbs the preterite and past participle forms are leveled to the form of the present, eliminating all tense inflection. In a small group ending in /-t/, *knit*, *fit*, and *sweat*, this usage should be classed as standard, to judge from our survey. In another group the uninflected forms have more or less currency in popular but not in cultured speech: *give*, *run*, *eat*, *come*, *see*, *ask*, *sit*, and *set* 'sat.' Still other uninflected preterites or past participles are entirely, or almost entirely, limited to a few Negro informants: *rise*, *drive*, *bring*, *throw*, *take*, *drink*, *dive*, *climb*, and *wake*. With more complete data we might establish this feature as characteristic of primitive Negro speech; however, lack of inflection among such informants is often combined with syntactic peculiarities, as in *I done bring* and *Is you drink?*

Loss of the preterite affix /-t, -d, -əd/ in weak verbs is as a rule not common in popular speech. In addition to *ask* and the group with final /-t/ mentioned above, the affix is missing with regularity only in *dreamt*, which very frequently appears as /drɛmp/. The affix is apparently felt to be func-

tional and necessary; it is even added sometimes to strong verbs, as in *stoled*, *swoled*, *frozed*, *tored*, *tooked*, and *takened*. This type of form is not, however, very common.

A rather noticeable feature of popular usage is the disinclination to inflect for number—i.e., to distinguish between verb forms according to the number of the subject. This is particularly noticeable in the preterite of *to be: we was, you was,* and so on. Since *be* is the only English verb which preserves the singular-plural distinction in the preterite, leveling of forms would be inevitable in all but the most disciplined speech.

With regard to trends and future possibilities we may speak only with great reserve. The Atlas materials tell us pretty clearly that the present trend—one that will probably continue as long as the present social and economic situation prevails—is for the older popular forms to retreat before the march of universal education and the middle-class aversion to rusticity. In fact, by the time the complete Linguistic Atlas is published, it is very probable that some of the Type I forms will be considerably more rare than when the fieldworkers gathered them, and even a few of the Type II forms may have become somewhat old-fashioned. Nevertheless, many of the popular forms are thriving, and occasionally one of these forms, such as *dove* ('dived'), will no doubt succeed in resisting the combined influences of the schoolroom and the English of literature. Very often, of course, competition for respectability will continue between two forms, as *sweat* and *sweated*, *woke* and *waked*, *shrunk* and *shrank*, *dreamed* and *dreamt*, some of which are losing ground in one sector and gaining it in another. Even cultivated usage will probably never be entirely uniform, and regional preferences must always be considered in attempting to fix the standards of American usage.

---

[23] Some of the listings of the principal parts of verbs by H. L. Mencken, *The American Language* (New York: Knopf, 1936), pp. 427-36, imply that Mencken believes reversal of the standard forms to be regular in several verbs.

FIGURES 1-31

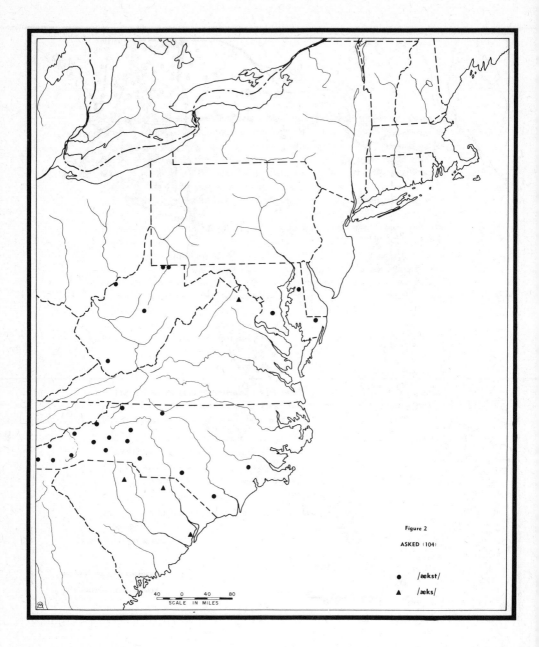

Figure 2

ASKED (104)

● /ækst/

▲ /æks/

SCALE IN MILES
40   0   40   80

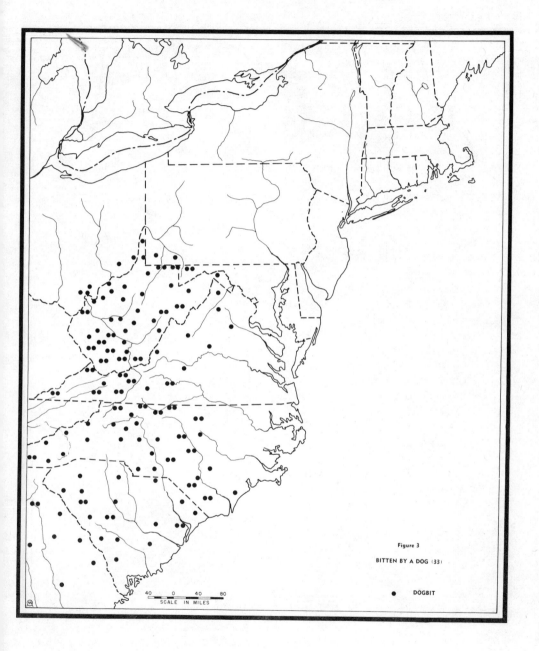

Figure 3

BITTEN BY A DOG (33)

● DOGBIT

40   0   40   80
SCALE IN MILES

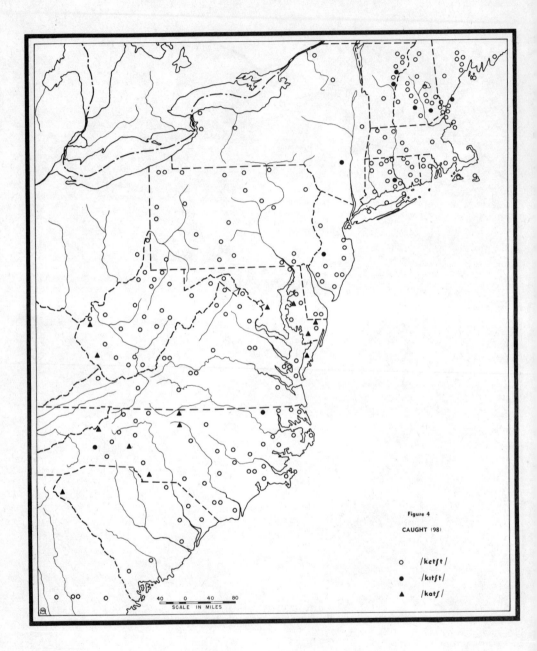

Figure 4

CAUGHT (98)

○ /kɛtʃt/

● /kɪtʃt/

▲ /katʃ/

SCALE IN MILES
40   0   40   80

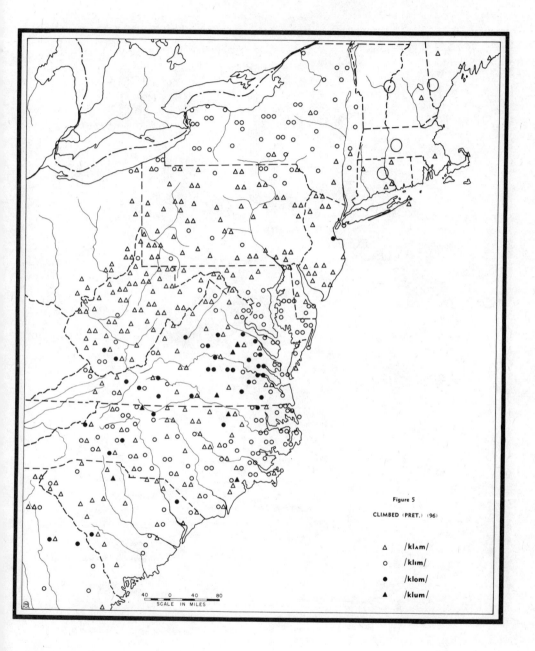

Figure 5

CLIMBED (PRET.) (96)

△ /klʌm/

○ /klɪm/

● /klom/

▲ /klum/

SCALE IN MILES
40   0   40   80

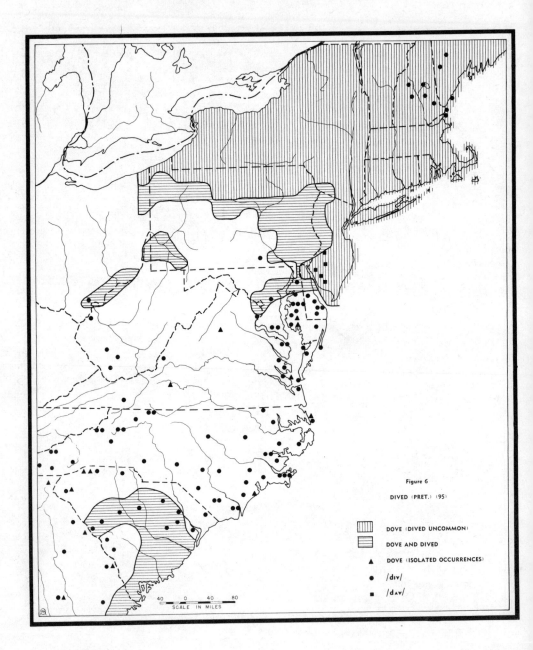

Figure 6

DIVED (PRET.) (95)

|||||| DOVE (DIVED UNCOMMON)

▭ DOVE AND DIVED

▲ DOVE (ISOLATED OCCURRENCES)

● /dɪv/

■ /dʌv/

40   0   40   80
SCALE IN MILES

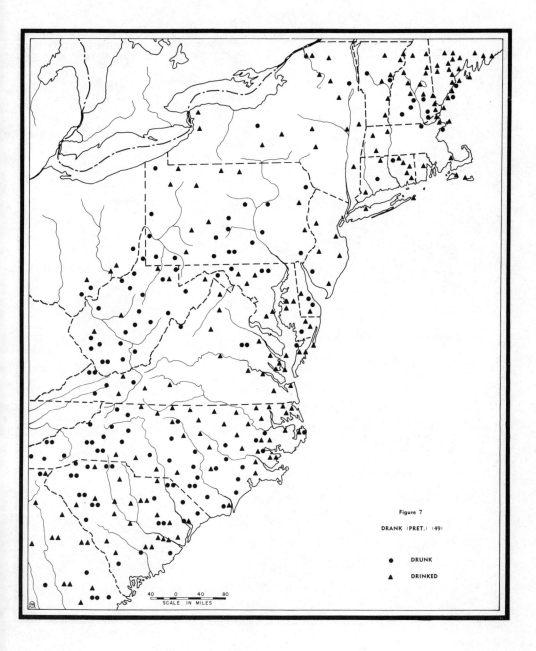

Figure 7

DRANK (PRET.) (49)

● DRUNK

▲ DRINKED

40   0   40   80
SCALE IN MILES

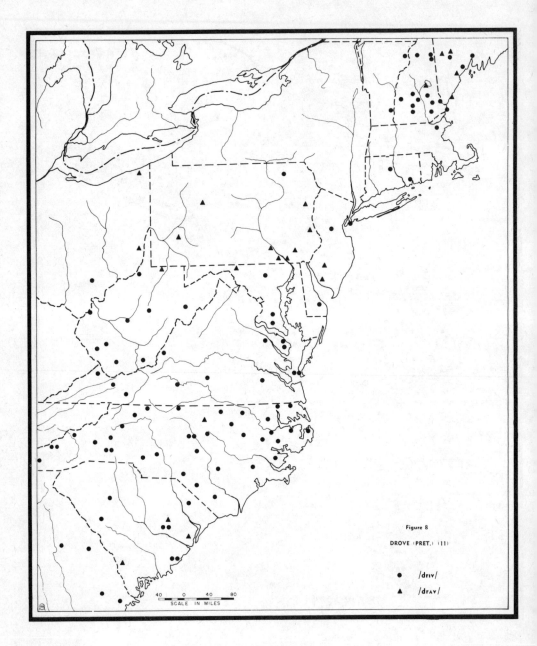

Figure 8

DROVE (PRET.) (11)

● /drɪv/

▲ /drʌv/

SCALE IN MILES

40   0   40   80

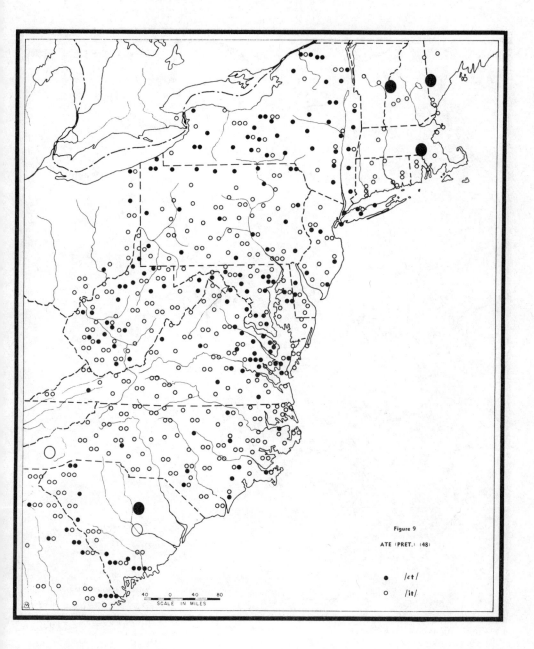

Figure 9

ATE (PRET.) (48)

● /ɛt/
○ /it/

SCALE IN MILES
40   0   40   80

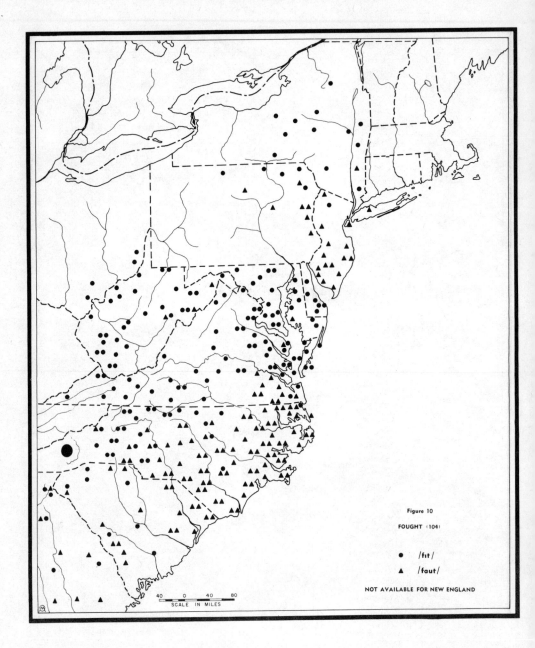

Figure 10

FOUGHT (104)

● /fɪt/

▲ /faut/

NOT AVAILABLE FOR NEW ENGLAND

40   0   40   80
SCALE IN MILES

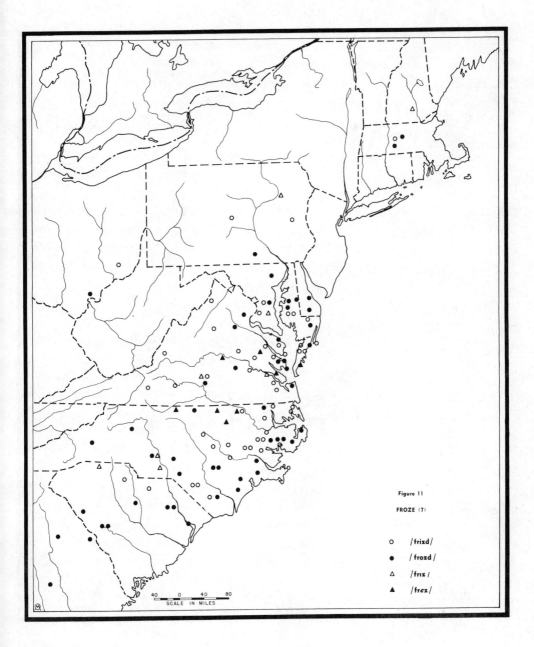

Figure 11

FROZE (7)

○ /frizd/

● /frozd/

△ /frɪz/

▲ /frɛz/

SCALE IN MILES
40 0 40 80

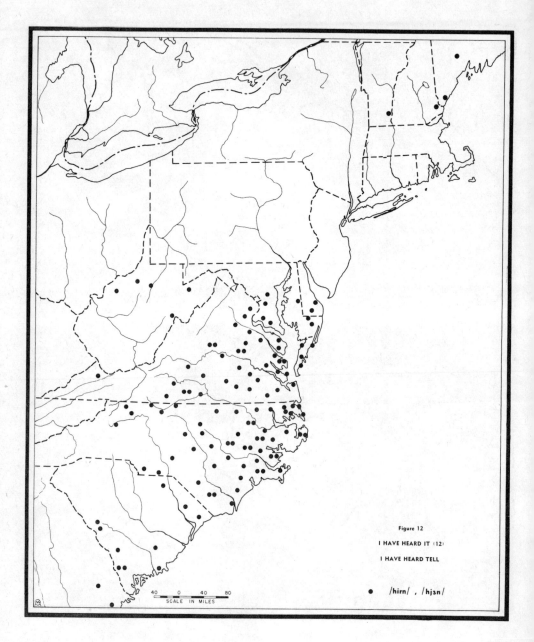

Figure 12

I HAVE HEARD IT (12)

I HAVE HEARD TELL

● /hirn/ , /hjɔn/

SCALE IN MILES
40   0   40   80

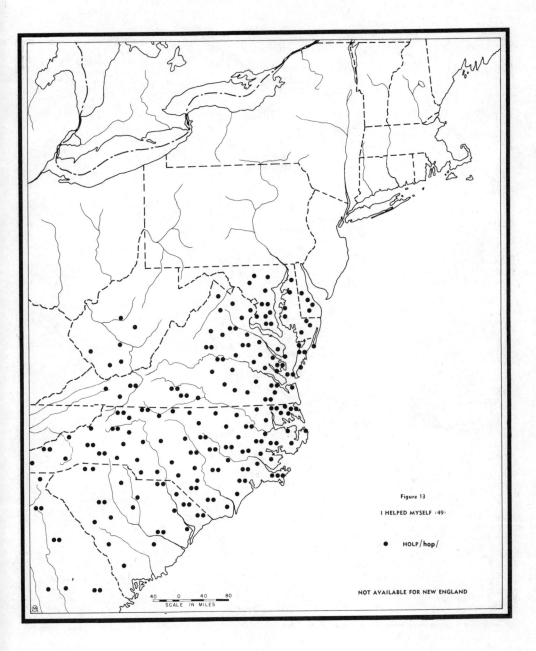

Figure 13

I HELPED MYSELF (49)

● HOLP /hop/

NOT AVAILABLE FOR NEW ENGLAND

40   0   40   80
SCALE IN MILES

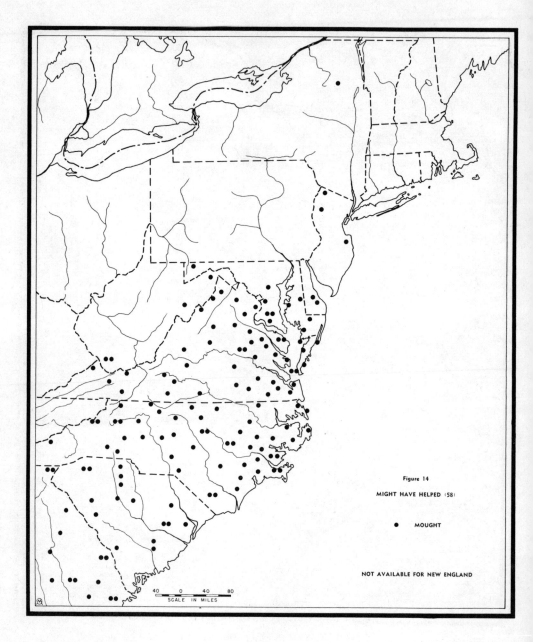

Figure 14

MIGHT HAVE HELPED (58)

● MOUGHT

NOT AVAILABLE FOR NEW ENGLAND

40   0   40   80
SCALE IN MILES

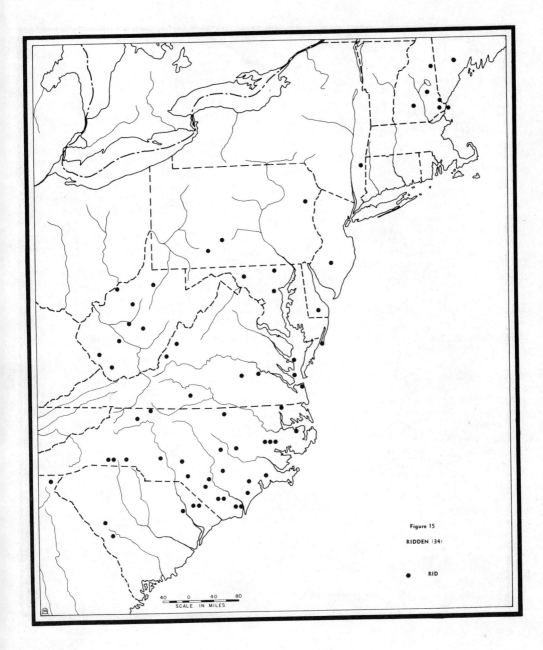

Figure 15

RIDDEN (34)

● RID

40 0 40 80
SCALE IN MILES

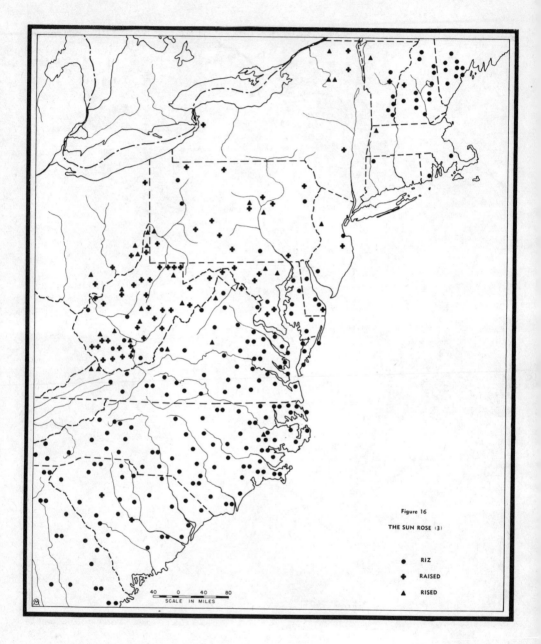

Figure 16

THE SUN ROSE (3)

● RIZ

✚ RAISED

▲ RISED

SCALE IN MILES
40 0 40 80

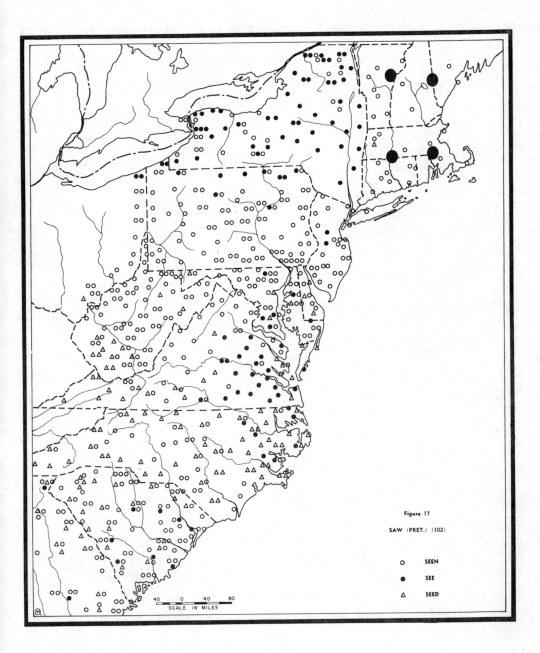

Figure 17

SAW (PRET.) (102)

○   SEEN

●   SEE

△   SEED

SCALE IN MILES
40   0   40   80

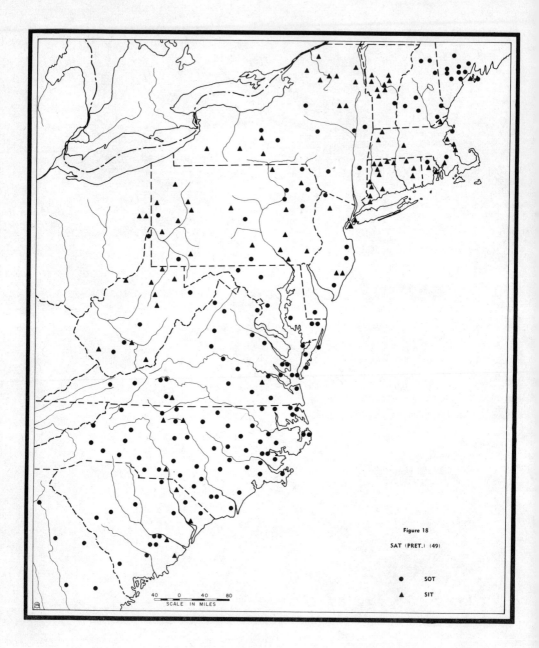

Figure 18

SAT (PRET.) (49)

● SOT

▲ SIT

SCALE IN MILES
40 0 40 80

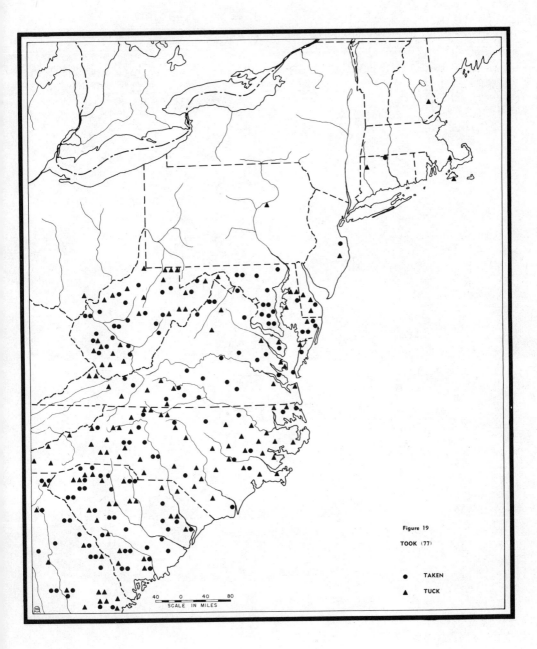

Figure 19

TOOK (77)

● TAKEN

▲ TUCK

40   0   40   80
SCALE IN MILES

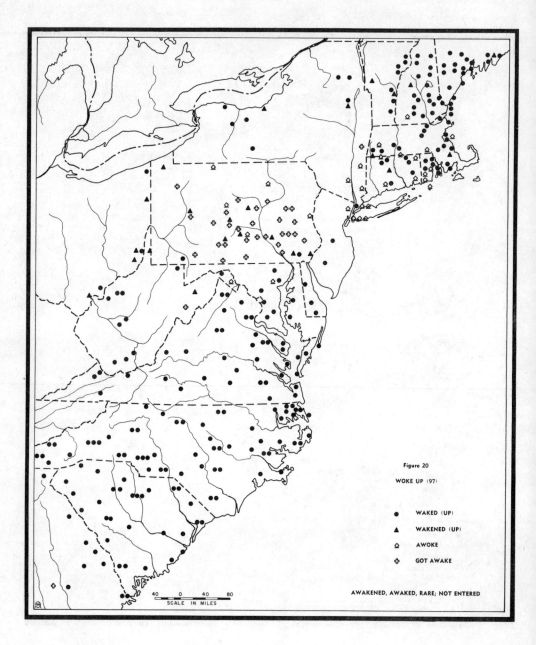

Figure 20

WOKE UP (97)

● WAKED (UP)

▲ WAKENED (UP)

✿ AWOKE

✤ GOT AWAKE

AWAKENED, AWAKED, RARE; NOT ENTERED

40   0   40   80
SCALE IN MILES

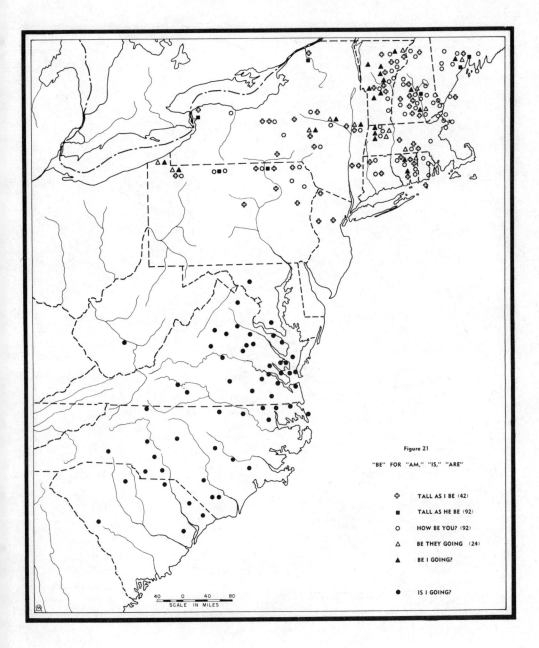

Figure 21

"BE" FOR "AM," "IS," "ARE"

✚	TALL AS I BE (42)
■	TALL AS HE BE (92)
○	HOW BE YOU? (92)
△	BE THEY GOING (24)
▲	BE I GOING?
●	IS I GOING?

40   0   40   80
SCALE IN MILES

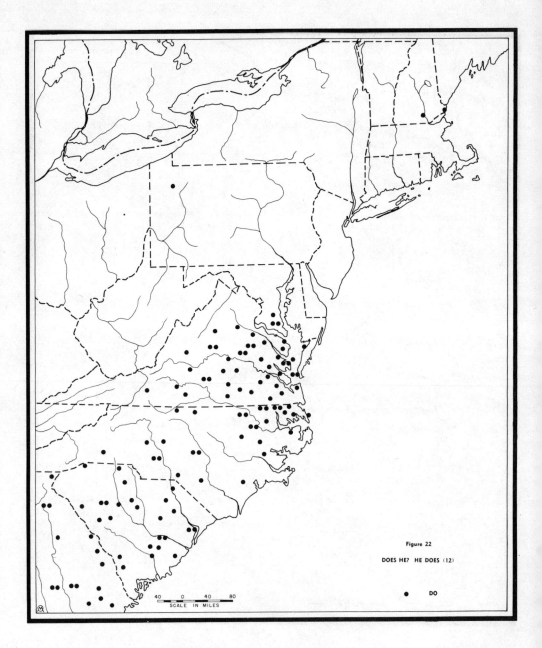

Figure 22

DOES HE? HE DOES (12)

● DO

40   0   40   80
SCALE IN MILES

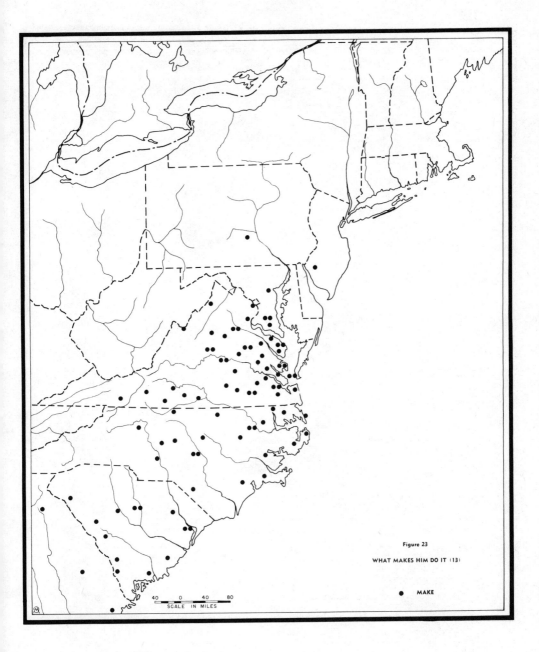

Figure 23

WHAT MAKES HIM DO IT (13)

• MAKE

40   0   40   80
SCALE IN MILES

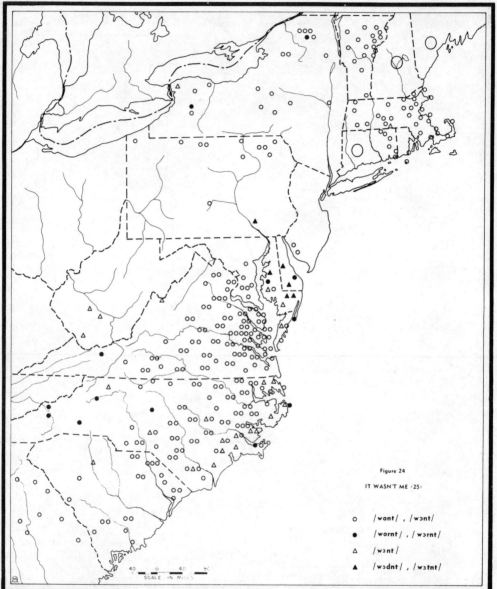

Figure 24

IT WASN'T ME (25)

○   /want/ , /wɔnt/

●   /warnt/ , /wɔrnt/

△   /wɜnt/

▲   /wɜdnt/ , /wɜtnt/

SCALE IN MILES

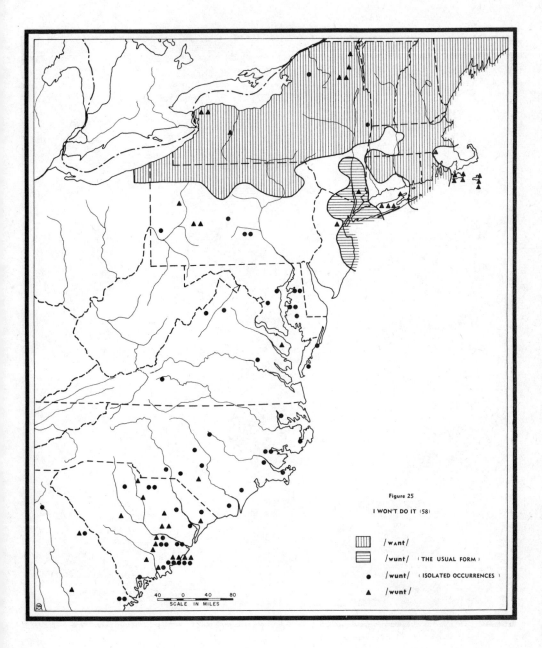

Figure 25

I WON'T DO IT (58)

/wʌnt/

/wunt/ (THE USUAL FORM)

/wunt/ (ISOLATED OCCURRENCES)

/wunt/

40   0   40   80
SCALE IN MILES

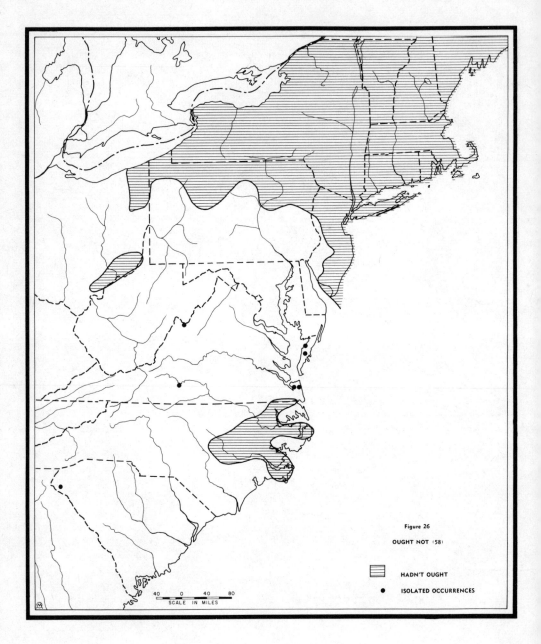

Figure 26

OUGHT NOT (58)

HADN'T OUGHT

● ISOLATED OCCURRENCES

40   0   40   80
SCALE IN MILES

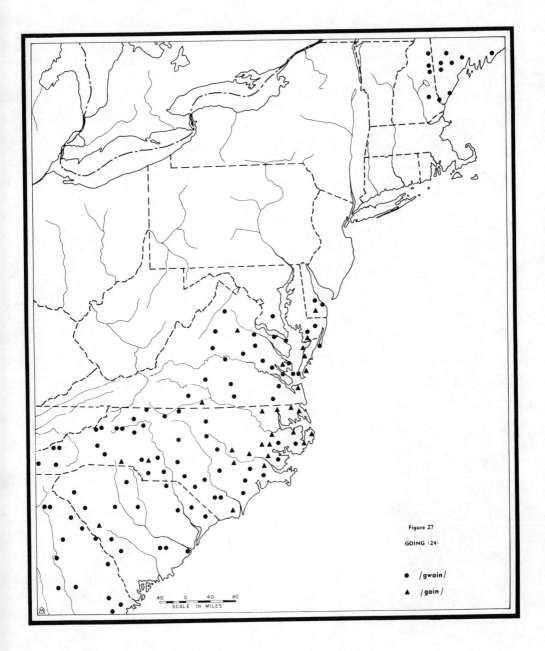

Figure 27

GOING (24)

● /gwain/

▲ /gain/

SCALE IN MILES
40   0   40   80

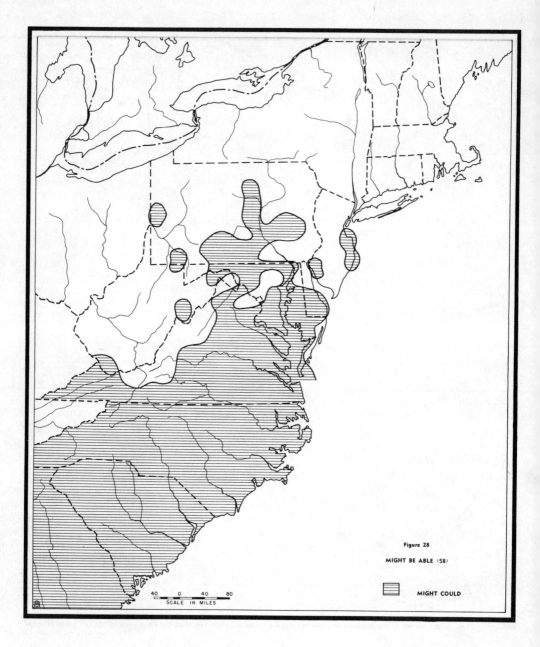

Figure 28

MIGHT BE ABLE (58)

MIGHT COULD

SCALE IN MILES
40   0   40   80

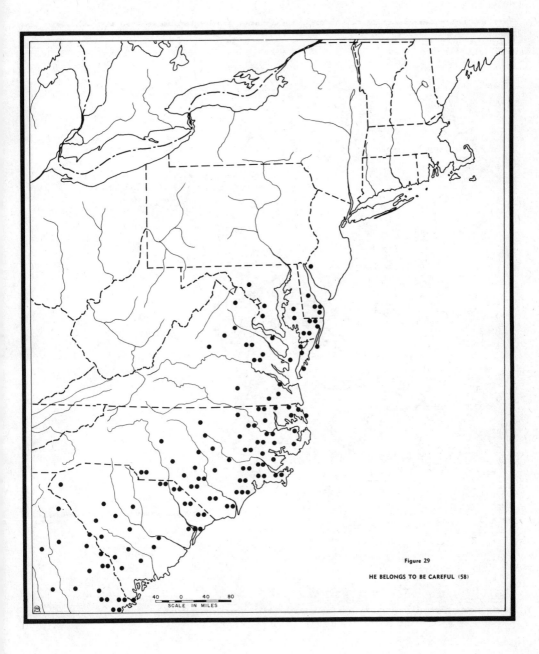

Figure 29

HE BELONGS TO BE CAREFUL (58)

SCALE IN MILES
40   0   40   80

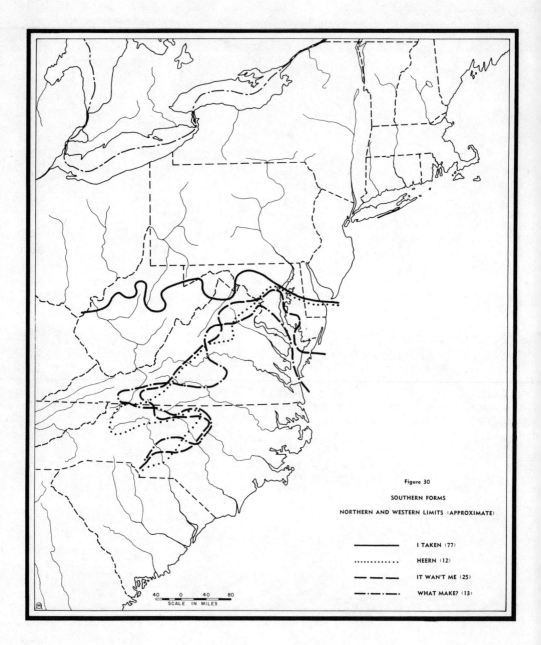

Figure 30

SOUTHERN FORMS

NORTHERN AND WESTERN LIMITS (APPROXIMATE)

I TAKEN (77)

HEERN (12)

IT WAN'T ME (25)

WHAT MAKE? (13)

SCALE IN MILES
40   0   40   80

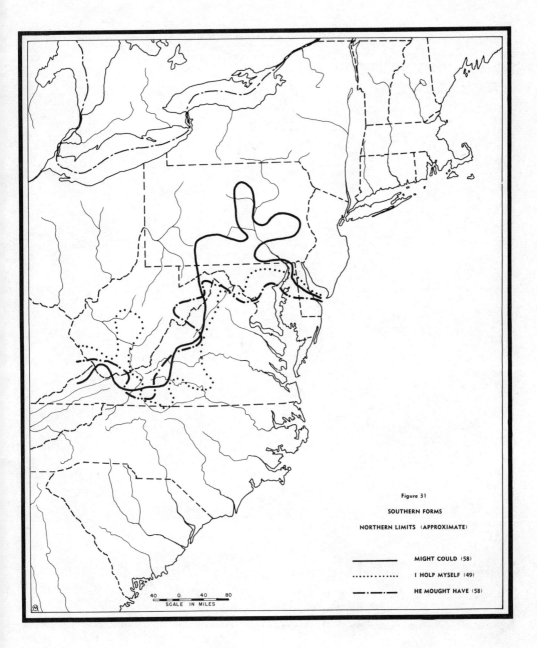

Figure 31

SOUTHERN FORMS

NORTHERN LIMITS (APPROXIMATE)

——————————— MIGHT COULD (58)

···················· I HOLP MYSELF (49)

—·——·——·—— HE MOUGHT HAVE (58)

SCALE IN MILES
40   0   40   80

INDEX OF FORMS

References are to pages. Phonemic symbols which are not also part of the conventional alphabet are alphabetized as follows: a, ɑ, æ; ch, tʃ; e, ɛ, ɜ, ə; i, ɪ; j, dʒ; n, ŋ; o, ɔ; sh, ʃ; th, θ; u, ʊ, ʌ. The abbreviation "ppl." used alone means 'past participle.'

Preterite and past participle variants are referred to the corresponding standard present infinitive forms in parentheses, thus: "Div (pret. of *dive*)." Since the present form was rarely entered in the field records, it is usually not possible to state positively that the standard present form would have been used by the informants. In very dubious cases, a query [?] appears. Variants in personal forms, negative forms, phrases, and so on, are referred to their standard equivalents in single quotation marks, thus: "Hadn't ought 'ought not,' " or "Make 'makes.' "

A

a-laughing (pres. ppl.) 34–35
a-singing (pres. ppl.) 34–35, 42
ain't 'am not' (neg. pres. 1st sg.) 30–31, 37, 41
ain't 'haven't' (neg. pres. 1st sg.) 31
am (pres. 1st sg.) 27, 38, 42
am not (neg. pres. 1st sg.) 30
am (I) not? (neg. pres. 1st sg.) 31, 37
are (pres. 2nd sg.) 27, 38, 42; (pres. 3rd pl.) 29–30
aren't 'am not' (neg. pres. 1st sg.) 31, 37
ask (inf.) 5; (pres.) 5; (pret.) 5, 44; (leveled pret. and ppl.) 44
asked (pret. of *ask*) 5, Fig. 2
ast (pres. of *ask*) 5; (pret.) 5
ate (pret. of *eat*) 12–13, Fig. 9; (ppl.) 13; (leveled pret. and ppl.) 13
awaked (pret. of *awake*[?]) 25
awakened (pret. of *awaken*[?]) 25
awoke (pret. of *awake*[?]) 25, Fig. 20
ax (pres. of *ask*) 5–6; (pret.) 5–6, Fig. 2
axed (pret. of *ax*) 5–6, 41, Fig. 2
/ær/ 'are' (pres. 2nd sg.) 27
/æs/ 'ask(ed)' (pres. and pret. of *ask*) 5

B

/bailt/ (ppl. of *boil*) 6
be (inf.) 27, 32, 44; (pres. indicative) 27, 38, 41, 42, Fig. 21
be 'am' (pres. 1st sg.) 27, 40, Fig. 21

be 'are' (pres. 2nd) 27; (pres. 3rd pl.) 27, Fig. 21
be 'is' (pres. 3rd sg.) 27, Fig. 21
begin (inf.) 6; (pret.) 6
begun (pret. of *begin*) 6, 42; (ppl.) 43
belong 'belongs' (pres. 3rd sg.) 35
belongs to be (pres. 3rd sg.) 35, 39, 40, Fig. 29
bit (pret. of *bite*) 42; (ppl.) 6, 41, 42
bite (inf.) 6; (pres.) 42; (ppl.) 6
bitten (ppl. of *bite*) 6
bled (pret. of *bleed*) 42
bleed (pres.) 42
blew (pret. of *blow*) 6
blow (inf.) 6
blowed (pret. of *blow*) 6, 38, 42
boil (inf.) 6
boiled (ppl. of *boil*) 6
boilt (ppl. of *boil*) 6, 39, 40, 41
bought (ppl. of *buy*) 7–8
boughten (ppl. of *buy*) 7–8, 37
break (inf.) 7
bring (inf.) 7; (pres.) 42; (leveled pret. and ppl.) 44
broke (ppl. of *break*) 7, 41, 43
broken (ppl. of *break*) 7
brought (ppl. of *bring*) 7
broughten (ppl. of *bring*) 7
brung (pret. of *bring*) 42; (ppl.) 7, 42
burst (inf.) 7; (pres.) 7; (pret.) 4, 7
bursted (pret. of *burst*) 7

hearn (ppl. of *hear*) 16
heat (inf.) 16; (pres.) 42
heated (ppl. of *heat*) 16
heen't 'haven't' (neg. pres. 1st sg.) 31
heered (pret. of *hear*) 40, 42; (ppl.) 16
heern (ppl. of *hear*) 16, 37, 40, 41, 42, Figs. 12, 30
help (inf.) 16
helped (pret. and ppl. of *help*) 16
het (pret. of *heat*) 42; (ppl.) 16, 42
/hɛv/ 'have' (pres. 1st sg.) 26
hid (pret. of *hide*) 42
hide (pres.) 42
/hird/ (ppl. of *hear*) 16
/hɪts/ 'there are' (pres. 3rd pl.) 30
/hjɜd/ (ppl. of *hear*) 16
/hjɜn/ (ppl. of *hear*) 16, Fig. 12
holp (pret. of *help*) 16–17, 40, 41, 42; (leveled pret. and ppl.) 16–17, 39, Figs. 13, 31
holped (pret. of *help*) 17
hung (ppl. of *hang*) 16, 41

I

is 'am' (pres. 1st sg.) 27, 39, 40, 41
is 'are' (pres. 2nd sg.) 27, 44; (pres. 3rd pl.) 27, 30, 41
is (pres. 3rd sg.) 38, 42

K

/kɛtʃt/ (pret. of *catch*) 8, Fig. 4
/kɪtʃt/ (pret. of *catch*) 8, Fig. 4
/klɪm/ (pres. of *climb*) 43
/klɪmd/ (pret. of *clim*) 43
kneed (pret. of *kneel*[?]) 17
kneel (inf.) 17; (pret.) 17
kneeled (pret. of *kneel*) 17, 41
kneened (pret. of *kneel*[?]) 17
knelt (pret. of *kneel*) 17
knew (pret. of *know*) 17
knit (inf.) 17; (pret.) 17, 41; (leveled pret. and ppl.) 44
knitted (pret. of *knit*) 17
know (inf.) 17; (pret.) 17
knowed (pret. of *know*) 17, 41, 42
known (pret. of *know*) 17
/kɔs/ 'costs' (pres. 3rd sg.) 28
/kɔsəz/ 'costs' (pres. 3rd sg.) 28
/kɔstəz/ 'costs' (pres. 3rd sg.) 28

L

laid (pret. of *lie* or *lay*) 18, 41
lay (pres.) 18; (pret.) 18
/læfɪn/ 'laughing' (pres. ppl.) 34
lead (pres.) 42
learn (inf.) 17
learn 'teach' (inf.) 24
learned (pret. of *learn*) 17–18
learnt (pret. of *learn*) 17–18
led (pret. of *lead*) 42
lie (inf.) 18; (pres.) 18; (pret.) 18
lied (pret. of *lie*) 18
like to fell 'almost fell' (pret. 1st sg.) 36, 41
like to have fallen 'almost fell' (pret. 1st sg.) 36
long 'belongs to be' (pres. 3rd sg.) 35
longs 'belongs to be' (pres. 3rd sg.) 35
look like 'looks like' (pres. 3rd sg.) 28
looks (pres. 3rd sg.) 28

M

(I)'m 'I have' (pres. 1st sg.) 26–27, 41, 42
(I)'m not 'am not' (neg. pres. 1st sg.) 30, 31, 35
make 'makes' (pres. 3rd sg.) 28, 39, 40, 41, Figs. 23, 30
makes (pres. 3rd sg.) 28
/mɛk/ 'makes' (pres. 3rd sg.) 28
might (pret. of *may*[?]) 18, 35
might could 'might be able' (future) 18, 35, 39, 40, 41, Figs. 28, 31
mought 'might' (pret.) 3, 18, 35, 39, 40, 41, 42, Figs. 14, 31

N

never used to 'didn't use to' (neg. pret. 3rd sg.) 34

O

ought (3rd sg.) 32
ought not (neg. 3rd sg.) 32–33
oughtn't (neg. 3rd sg.) 33
/ɔrtnt/ 'oughtn't' (neg. 3rd sg.) 33

P

plead (inf.) 18–19; (pres.) 42
pleaded (pret. of *plead*) 19
pled (pret. of *plead*) 18–19, 41, 42

swum (pret. of *swim*) 23, 42, 43; (leveled pret.
 and ppl.) 43
swunk (pret. of *shrink* or *swink*) 21; (ppl.) 21
/swʊld/ (pret. of *swell*) 22

T

take (inf.) 23, 43; (pret.) 24; (ppl.) 24; (leveled pret. and ppl.) 44
taked (pret. of *take*) 24
taken (pret. of *take*) 24, 40, 41, 43, Figs. 19, 30;
 (ppl.) 24, 43; (leveled pret. and ppl.) 24, 43
takened (pret. of *take*) 24, 44; (ppl.) 24; (leveled
 pret. and ppl.) 24
takes after 'looks like' (pres. 3rd sg.) 28
taught (pret. of *teach*) 24
teach (inf.) 24
teached (pret. of *teach*) 24, 41, 42
tear (inf.) 24; (ppl.) 24
tell (inf.) 34
think (pres. 3rd pl.) 29, 39
thinks 'think' (pres. 3rd pl.) 29, 39, 41
threw (pret. of *throw*) 24
throw (inf.) 24; (pret.) 25, 44
throwed (pret. of *throw*) 25, 38, 41, 42
thrown (pret. of *throw*) 25
/θod/ (pret. of *throw*) 25
toke (pret. of *take*) 24
took (pret. of *take*) 23–24; (ppl.) 24; (leveled
 pret. and ppl.) 24
tooked (pret. of *take*) 24, 44
tooken (pret. of *take*) 24; (ppl.) 24
tore (ppl. of *tear*) 24, 41
tored (ppl. of *tear*) 24, 44
torn (ppl. of *tear*) 24
/tɔr/ 'torn' (ppl. of *tear*) 24
tuck (pret. of *take*) 23–24, 40, 41, 43, Fig. 19;
 (ppl.) 24, 40, 43; (leveled pret. and ppl.) 24, 43

U

used not to (be) 'didn't use to' (neg. pret. 3rd sg.)
 34
used to (pret. 3rd sg.) 33
used to (be) not 'didn't use to' (neg. pret. 3rd
 sg.) 34
used to didn't 'didn't use to' (neg. pret. 3rd sg.) 34
used to not (be) 'didn't use to' (neg. pret. 3rd sg.)
 34
used to wan't 'didn't use to' (neg. pret. 3rd sg.) 34

used to wuzn't 'didn't use to' (neg. pret. 3rd sg.)
 34
usen't 'didn't use to' (neg. pret. 3rd sg.) 33

V

(I)'ve 'have' (pres. 1st sg.) 26
(I)'ve got 'have' (pres. 1st sg.) 26

W

wake (inf.) 25; (pret.) 25, 44
waked (pret. of *wake*) 25, 38, 40, 44, Fig. 20
wakened (pret. of *wake* or *waken*) 25, Fig. 20
wan't 'was not' (neg. pret. 3rd sg.) 32, 38, 39, 40,
 41, Figs. 24, 30
wan't used to (be) 'didn't use to' (neg. pret. 3rd
 sg.) 34
warmed (ppl. of *warm*) 16
warn't 'was not' (neg. pret. 3rd sg.) 32, Fig. 24
was 'were' (pret. 2nd sg.) 28–29, 41, 42, 44;
 (pret. 1st pl.) 29, 41, 44
was not (neg. pret. 3rd sg.) 32
wasn't (neg. pret. 3rd sg.) 38
/wɑdənt/ 'was not' (neg. pret. 3rd sg.) 32
wear (inf.) 25
werdn't 'was not' (neg. pret. 3rd sg.) 32, 42, Fig.
 24
were (pret. 2nd sg.) 28–29, 41; (pret. 1st pl.) 29
weren't 'was not' (neg. pret. 3rd sg.) 32, Fig. 24
/wɜtnt/ 'was not' (neg. pret. 3rd sg.) 32, Fig. 24
will not (neg. pres. 1st sg.) 32
woke (pret. of *wake*) 25, 44
woked (pret. of *wake*) 25
woken (pret. of *wake*) 25
/wont/ 'was not' (neg. pret. 3rd sg.) 32
won't 'will not' (neg. pres. 1st sg.) 32, 38
/wont/ 'will not' (neg. pres. 1st sg.) 32
wore (ppl. of *wear*) 25, 38, 41, 43
work (pres. 1st sg. and pl.) 26
works 'work' (pres. 1st sg.) 26; (pres. 1st pl.) 26,
 41; (pres. 3rd pl.) 26
worn (ppl. of *wear*) 25
/wɔnt/ 'was not' (neg. pret. 3rd sg.) 32
/wɔnt/ 'will not' (neg. pres. 1st. sg.) 32
/wɔr/ (ppl. of *wear*) 25
/wɔrn/ (ppl. of *wear*) 25
/wɔrnt/ 'was not' (neg. pret. 3rd sg.) 32, Fig. 24
writ (pret. of *write*) 42; (ppl.) 26, 42
write (inf.) 26; (pres.) 42; (ppl.) 26